The Mystic Experience

The SUNY series in Religious Studies
edited by Harold Coward

The Mystic Experience

A Descriptive and Comparative Analysis

Jordan Paper

State University of New York Press

Published by
State University of New York Press, Albany

For information, address State University of New York Press,
90 State Street, Suite 700, ALbany, NY 12207

Production by Kelli Williams
Marketing by Michael Campochiaro

Library of Congress Cataloging-in-Publication Data

Paper, Jordan D.
    The mystic experience: a descriptive and comparative analysis / Jordan Paper.
        p. cm. — (SUNY series in religious studies)
    Includes bibliographical references and index.
    ISBN 0-7914-6249-7 (hc : alk. paper)—ISBN 0-7914-6250-1 (pbk : alk. paper)
        1. Mysticism.   I. Title.

BL625.P365   2004
204'.22—dc22

                                                                    2003068695

10 9 8 7 6 5 4 3 2 1

To the grandfather after whom I am named and, accordingly, never met, and whom, I have been told, I resemble more than just physically.

—Yeshua ben Yosef (Jordan Paper)

Contents

Preface

Concerning the topic of this book, the mystic, zero, or void-experience, over many years much has been written about essentially nothing. But paradox is generally acknowledged to be one of the features of the experience, which is the ecstatic disappearance of self along with everything else. Rather than a nihilistic experience, it is one that invariably is considered by those who have had it to be the most beautiful, blissful, positive, profound, and significant experience(s) of their lives. But given the many tomes that exist on the topic, why another book? Is there anything new to be expressed?

Most of the books written on the subject have been from a Christian theological perspective or have focused on its appearance in a particular religious tradition, such as Hinduism. Studies have been written from a variety of academic disciplines, but exceedingly few from the standpoint of comparative religion. There are a number of works that attempt to be comparative, but they tend to be compendiums of various statements of experience from a number of religious traditions without being methodologically comparative. Isolating out a number of possible common factors is not in and of itself comparative, as this approach does not probe cultural meanings. A failing of all but a few studies is the distancing of the author from the experience itself. Many authors make a point of their not understanding the phenomenon, which raises the concern as to why, of all people, they are writing about it.

The sole prominent exception to the last point is the work by the late anthropologist and self-avowed mystic, Agehananda Bharati, who begins his study with his own experience. But, as the work primarily concerns Hinduism, it is of limited comparative usefulness. By example, Bharati taught me, a comparative religionist, to come out of the closet with regard to personal ecstatic experience over two decades ago, and I begin and end this work with my own experiences.

These experiences and those self-recorded by individuals who did not necessarily link their experience with any religious tradition or provide an interpretive framework are compared to draft the characteristics of a universal human experience prior to the imposition of cultural interpretive frameworks. These characteristics are then compared to statements of acknowledged mystics in a number of traditions for corroboration. The mystic experience is subsequently situated within the gestalt of ecstatic religious experiences to delineate it from other, sometimes seemingly similar, ones. This is the procedure utilized for the descriptive (phenomenological) analysis.

After an analytical survey of the literature on the subject from a number of disciplinary approaches, this study then shifts into the comparative mode. Using the methods of religio-ecology—studying religion with regard to all of the factors that influence the culture and the specific phenomenon being studied—and ethnohermeneutics—focusing on what is most significant within specific cultures, on how cultures fundamentally understand life and the world around them—a variety of cultures around the world, not just religions, are studied to understand how the mystic experience is variously interpreted and integrated into cultures, past and present.

From these dual approaches, it is possible to more fully comprehend the mystic experience as both a human and a cultural experience. This is the only study to date to so analyze the mystic experience.

Acknowledgments

As with any study that is based on decades of research and reflection, it would be impossible to acknowledge all those who have, in various ways, contributed to this work. Particularly influential on my understanding of the phenomenology and hermeneutics of the mystic experience are conversations with the late anthropologist and tantric Hindu guru, Agehananda Bharati; the Buddhist scholar-monk, Mingfu Fashi; the master medium, You Meilin; the Daoist monk, Mo Daoren; a Sufi master I met in Konya; the scholar of Jewish mysticism, Elliot Wolfson; and the scholar of Islamic mysticism, Michael Sells; as well as the shaman Marilyn Johnson, Dan Merkur, Aviva Goldberg, and other former students, undergraduate as well as graduate. Of course, this does not necessarily mean that those with whom I discussed the mystic experience would necessarily agree with all of my views. I am also grateful for suggestions from the readers to whom the State University of New York Press sent the initial manuscript.

With regard to the research specific to this work, I am indebted to the Religious Experience Research Centre, then housed at Westminster College in Oxford (and now at the University of Wales in Lampeter), and the former director, Peggy Morgan, for her congenial hospitality and permission to reproduce extracts from the archives that form a substantial part of chapter 2. A research grant from the Faculty of Arts and a sabbatical supplement grant from the Senate of York University partially supported my travel to Turkey, England, China, Taiwan, and the United States while carrying out specific research for this work between 1999 and 2001. The Centre for Studies in Religion and Society of the University of Victoria has offered collegial and logistic support for this study since 1999.

As I have been writing on this topic for well over a quarter century, various bits and pieces of this work have been previously published, although most of these have been substantially modified and are acknowledged in passing and referenced. Nonetheless, the preponderance of this work is entirely new.

1

Introduction

AN EVENT

In 1972, the most momentous event of my life took place on a perfect summer day at an ideal summer occasion, a weekend folk music/jazz festival on the beautiful park-island that forms the outer boundary of Toronto's harbor. I was assisting a newly befriended couple who crafted leather bags and were selling them from their pushcart, and had met through them that morning a female artist who, with her husband, have remained my closest friends since. It was early afternoon and, having finished a light lunch, I lay down alone on the grass under the shade of an old tree.

I was lying on my side and directly in my vision across a sunlit, mown field I perceived an attractive woman. Without moving my head or eyes, I focused on her, enjoying the vision with little or no thought, save a pleasant erotic feeling. At first she slowly filled my vision, as if I were floating toward her or her toward me. Then with increasing speed she came closer and closer, followed by trees, rocks, the field, then the entire universe, whirling in a giant vortex that funneled into me. As everything literally became one with me, I perceived a bright light inside rather than outside of me. This light can best be described as white, but it was all colors simultaneously, and it was bright beyond the brightest light imaginable. I, the universe, began to fly faster and faster toward this light. At that moment, I comprehended that I had to make an instantaneous decision: I could enter the light into which I would merge and be gone or stop and end the experience. Somehow, I recognized what was happening; I sped into the light and dissolved in an immense flood tide of joy.

Later—it could have been a quarter of an hour or an hour or more—I regained awareness. At first I was but aware of a blissful nothingness; that is, the first awareness was simply of being aware while awash in the afterglow of bliss. Then there was an awareness of a somethingness, which I began to perceive as composed of things: sensations of sights and sounds. Slowly these components took on specific qualities, took on names and meanings. The world was again around me; there was an "I" that was again in a remembered world. But it was not the same "I" as before. It was an "I" that knew with absolute certitude that the state of being an "I" was less true than the state of being not "I," that the only reality is a blissful, utterly undifferentiated nothingness in which there is no "I."

As soon as I was again, that is, existing as a self-conscious, distinct entity, still not having moved, my readings of the *Zhuangzi* and the *Daodejing*, and of various Chan Buddhist texts came to the forefront of my consciousness. I realized I had just experienced the primordial nothingness becoming a oneness; the oneness distinguished into a twoness; the twoness becoming the myriad things. I truly understood *ziran* (spontaneity/nature), for I had just recreated myself and the world around me. Death could never again be a mystery, for I had experienced not-being. From the second perspective, I had just experienced *wuxin* (no-mind) or *śūnyatā* (emptiness). Echoes of Meister Eckhart and the extant writings of other well-known mystics, unbidden, reverberated in my head.

As I begin the initial chapter of this book, this is the first time I have ever put this memory into writing. But this memory is different from all other memories that I have, save the few related ones, for it always remained far more than a vivid memory, or nonmemory to be precise. The experience is perpetually alive for me as if it has just happened.

Soon after, I began to reflect on the factors of my life that, if they did not generate the experience, at least created the circumstances that allowed for it to happen. This was important to know, if the experience were to be repeated. And after that experience, there was none other worth repeating.

Indeed, my circumstances were unusual. I had moved to Toronto from a small southern Indiana city a month previous to take up a new university post. I had gone from an area where I was a despised minority—in several ways—to what is still considered one of the finest and most metropolitan cities in the world. I had left behind a place into which I could not fit, a dead marriage, and a deadening scholarly direction for a vibrant artistic world, new social opportunities, and a return to the only scholarly direction that excited me—religious studies. I was physically fit, taking up again in Toronto *kendo* and *iaido* (Japanese swordsmanship of two types) in which I had not been able to engage since leaving Kyoto years before. I had returned to a simple semivegetarian diet. I had no emotional entanglements. I had not yet begun to teach or do research in my new intellectual direction. I had just bought a small island with a one-room cabin a few hours north of Toronto that was to remain my home for the next sixteen years and was but awaiting the paperwork to be completed so I could move in. It was a still point in a life.

Perhaps a pleasant, positive, vacuous life is conducive to an experience of the void. After all, this is the environment that many Buddhist and Christian contemplative monasteries seek to create. For myself, I hoped to eventually remarry and was looking forward to the challenges of creative teaching and research, as well as an active academic career, all of which would inevitably engender frustration and other negative factors, along with positive ones. Although I knew that this experience was the only utterly meaningful (or meaningless) experience of my life, and I would certainly welcome absolute joy were it to occur again, I would not reorder my life to encourage its reoccurrence. I chose to plunge back into the world of illusion; to have had the experience once is sufficient for a lifetime.

GENERAL CHARACTERISTICS OF THE "EVENT"

A perusal of similar self-reports (see chapter 2) allows a listing of common features of the previously described event, a list compatible with similar listings by other sympathetic scholars. These features in turn can be utilized to describe an experience that can be named. The common characteristics include the following:

I. Sequence of events:

   A. Person prior to experience, either
      1. still
      2. or moving in routinized movements/tasks that do not require conscious attention

   B. Feeling of merging/unity in several modes:
      1. feeling of slow to rapid expansion and joining with all
      2. or feeling of slow to rapid drawing of everything into oneself
         a. difference may be one of explanation rather than experiential

    C. Feeling of merging with light (common but not essential) with following usual characteristics:
       1. light either comes down to one or one rises to it
       2. light is deemed colorless or white
       3. light is intensely bright but not painful or uncomfortable
       4. there is full awareness that this is not physical light
       5. merging with light, at first slow, becoming rapid

    D. Self disappears with full merging/unity with all and/or light;
       1. *complete disappearance of self primary characteristic of experience*

    E. Awareness of being able to stop sequence before self disappears;
       1. hence, loss of self voluntary:
          a. experience understood to be highly positive and desirable
          b. events may or may not be interpreted prior to loss of self

    F. Slow, becoming rapid, reawareness after disappearance of self, usually in following order:
       1. reawareness of regaining of self
       2. reawareness of end of unity
       3. reawareness of distinction of things

    G. Interpretation of events immediately preceding experience
       1. tends to be based on previously learned/enculturated understandings
       2. and tends to reinforce these understandings

    H. Understanding that self disappeared due to following:
       1. memory of events just prior to experience
       2. and consciousness of regaining awareness from state of lack of awareness

II. Effects of experience are universally as follows:

    A. An understanding that what was experienced was more real/important than any prior experience

    B. An understanding that what was experienced either
       1. brings into question all that was known before
       2. or confirms theological or metaphysical/epistemological understandings

III. The experience lacks the following effects:

    A. there is no *necessary* change in personality or behavior

    B. the majority of those who have the experience do not communicate it to others, at least immediately

        1. hence, the experience does not usually lead to religious leadership and so forth

    C. the experience is not necessarily understood as religious or spiritual but it is understood as utterly profound

A NAME FOR THE EXPERIENCE

The experience discussed in this study has been termed by an anthropologist as the "zero-experience" and by some psychologists as the "void-experience." Both descriptive names are meaningful to those who have some understanding of the experience, but can be confusing to those unaware of it. A more direct term specific to the experience would be advantageous.

The Greek word *mustikos* and the Latin word *mysticus*, from which the English word "mystic" is derived, designate a person initiated into the Hellenistic (the generalized Greek-speaking culture prevalent among the educated throughout the eastern Mediterranean area from nineteen to twenty-three hundred years ago) esoteric religious cults into which most of the educated of the time were initiated. These initiations, although never directly revealed, suggest that the initiates had visions of the relevant deity after ingesting psychoactive substances (see Wasson et al.; Merkur, *The Mystery*), which is not the ecstasy previously delineated.

In contemporary popular parlance, the word "mystic" is used in manifold ways; for example, some large North American cities have an annual "Mystics and Seers Fair," or an equivalent, at an exhibition hall. Commercial ventures designed to part gullible individuals from their money are not the subject of this study either. *The Concise Oxford Dictionary* provides a more specific contemporary definition of "mystic." As a noun, the word is given the following meanings: "a person who seeks by contemplation and self-surrender to obtain unity or identity with or absorption into the Deity or the ultimate reality, or who believes in the spiritual apprehension of truths that are beyond the understanding."

Clearly, the modern meanings of "mystic" are rather different from their Hellenistic precursors. Focusing on the first aspect of the *Oxford* definition, I have termed the above described event as the "mystic experience," that is, that experience, as described in detail and outlined either, which mystics have or seek to have, regardless of method or lack of one. Avoiding the more all-encompassing term, "mysticism," this book is about the *mystic experience*.

THE MYSTIC EXPERIENCE IN CULTURAL CONTEXT

Ever since I have been teaching university courses on ecstatic religious experience, I have been approached by students who have had such experiences, particularly the mystic experience. (There are nuances to the experience that make it quite clear to one who has had the experience whether an experience being described is, indeed, the mystic experience.) At least 10 percent of students who have taken my course, "Mysticism," over the last two decades have had the experience, although it must be noted that the very nature of the course is to a degree self-selecting. Hence, it has become clear to me that such an experience is far from unusual. It has been argued that human beings by their very nature seek ecstatic experience—a viewpoint with which I am sympathetic—and everyone has ecstatic experiences, although they may not recognize or may deny them. Although an experience of the kind previously described is not universal to all humans, all humans do have nonordinary consciousness experiences, which, of course, include dreams. Chapter 2 will provide a number of self-descriptions of the mystic experience.

Some of these descriptions will be from major figures in religious traditions, some from the literature, and some from nonpublished self-reports. Although the mystic experience is universally acknowledged as ineffable, as with my own experience, descriptions of the experiences immediately preceding and following the mystic experience are available. The material in chapter 2 will focus on descriptions rather than interpretations, or, where feasible, will attempt to extract description from interpretation.

With a very few exceptions, the voluminous literature concerning the mystic experience renders its understanding extremely difficult. One problem is the tendency to conflate all ecstatic religious experiences under the rubric of "mysticism." The Greek word *musterion* and the Latin word *mysterium* specifically refer to the secret initiation rituals of the Hellenistic cults mentioned earlier. Although over the centuries perhaps hundreds of thousands of individuals were initiated into these cults, and many were initiated into several, the experiences were so profound that not a single description of any of these secret rituals has come down to us.

In contrast, nowadays, "mysticism" has come to mean simply anything that is mysterious (which also derives from the Greek and Latin words), particularly any mode of nonordinary mental functioning, as well as anything considered strange or unusual. Hence, the experience of no-self is lumped together with shamanistic and mediumistic (spirit possession) experiences, visions, lucid dreaming, prophecy, and the many modes of unitive experiences. In the contemporary understanding, legendary locales, such as Atlantis, and alien abduction and related phenomena are also subsumed under the term "mysticism." The many types of ecstatic religious experiences will be discussed, delineated, and compared in chapter 3.

Since the eighteenth-century European Enlightenment, nonconscious modes of thinking, as well as any thoughts derived from religious experiences, have been disparaged. Deemed irrational, such forms of mental behavior are to be avoided by all right-thinking persons. Yet most major breakthroughs in the sciences are due, as in the creative arts, to inspiration, that is subconscious mental processing. As humans, it is most unlikely that we have changed in the last several hundred years. Rather, what we have done in Western European culture (the Enlightenment did not strongly influence Eastern European culture, given Eastern Orthodoxy's stress on ecstatic religious experiences) is reduce what had been a variety of useful mental modes of functioning to a single acceptable one, that is, conscious reasoning. Accordingly, we have sharply curtailed culturally accepted mental behaviors, including several considered important, if not essential, in virtually all other cultures. Given the nature of the previously described experience, the Enlightenment could be understood as indicating the opposite, in that it denies the "light," the focus of the original meaning of "enlightenment," deriving from being "enlightened": one who receives or experiences the "light."

The contemporary manifestation of the Enlightenment's discomfort with nonordinary consciousness is found in most Western philosophical analyses of the experience under discussion. Many contemporary philosophers of religion have taken the position that an ineffable (indescribable) experience, that is, the mystic experience, is impossible, since we think in words, and a human experience that cannot be readily discussed could not happen. Moreover, all experiences whatsoever are culturally mediated; therefore, a universal human experience is also impossible. According to this line of reasoning, no one has had the mystic experience, and I and all others who claim to have had such an experience are either liars or deluded. Of course, for those who have had such an experience, this intellectual position is simply ridiculous. It is the equivalent of someone who is congenitally blind denying the existence of color. One can feel sorry for such an individual's limited experience, but how can one use that limited experience to determine that one's own experience never took place or is false? The history of studies of the experience will be the subject of chapter 4.

When I was an undergraduate psychology major in the late 1950s at the University of Chicago, I participated, in a most minor way, in the initial experiments on dream research. This research led to the realization of the commonality and universality of nonordinary mental states and decades of research by psychologists and neurologists on the workings of the brain in these regards. More recently, the term "neuroscience" has come into common parlance, indicating acceptance of mental functioning as neurophysiologically derived. Neuroscientists do not usually have a background in comparative religion and most of the interpretations in this regard to date have reflected either a confused understanding of ecstatic religious experiences or a tendency to posit Christian theological dogma as a neurophysiological reality. Chapter 4 will also explore the relevance of contemporary brain research, as well as research on near-death experiences, which tend to incorporate many features of the mystic experience.

The mystic experience is found in all religious traditions and in some is considered central to the religion, while in others, attempts are made to limit the experience to those within particular institutions because the experience is understood to threaten religious hierarchies. Chapters 5 and 6 will explore how a number of different traditions have interpreted and otherwise dealt with the experience.

The methodologies of chapters 5 and 6 will be that of ethnohermeneutics, the study of significance and meaning central to cultures, and religio-ecology, the analysis of religious phenomena with regard to all of the factors that impinge on a culture: inter and intracultural social and political relations, economic and technological development, geography, climate, and so forth. One of the fascinating aspects of the mystic experience within culture is the many ways in which the experience has been interpreted and understood. At times the understanding is so removed from the actual experience that it may actually be contrary to the experience itself. We will find not only theological interpretations but political ones as well; subsects of large religious traditions may take very different, if not opposite, attitudes toward the experience.

All of these studies will be brought together in chapter 7. In the concluding chapter, the interrelationships between different types of ecstatic experiences, as well as the history of the mystic experience in culture in general will be discussed. At the end, suggestions will be made regarding ways of understanding and relting oneself to the mystic experience.

A CAUTION TO READERS

As any human being, I can best understand experiences that I myself have experienced. Second best understood are the experiences of those whom I personally know and trust and who have shared their memories and realizations with me. Yet there is a tendency in the academic world to disparage self-referencing by scholars, particularly with regard to religious experience.

Scholarly objectivity is often understood to require distance from the studied topic. But does this make any sense? Why would an analysis of the mystic experience by someone who admittedly not only does not understand it but is doubtful about its actuality be more reliable than an analysis by someone who does know the experience? We do not expect scholars of the visual arts to be blind or of music to be deaf; indeed, we assume that a scholar of art enjoys the subject. I suggest there is a bias remaining from the Enlightenment in this regard, for it is only religious experience and no other that is handicapped by expectations of studies to be from those with no such experiences.

The first recognized Western scholar to openly describe and discuss his own experiences is Agehananda Bharati (see chapter 4). His example allowed others to come out of the closet. In previous publications, stimulated by Bharati, I have but hinted at my own experiences with regard to shamanism and the mystic experience. In this publication, for the first time, I fully follow Bharati's example and begin and end the study with reference to my own experiences. Only now, as I approach retirement, do I feel I have the scholarly maturity to deal with the subject in this manner. If self-reference, however, is found to be annoying, then this is not the book for you. Moreover, I am not neutral regarding these experiences. A reader of this manuscript suggested I read a recent study by Kripal, where I found an apt description of my own approach: "These are types of understandings that are at once passionate and critical, personal and objective, religious and academic"(5). Thus, the reader is forewarned.

Furthermore, as pointed out by reviewers of my previous books relating to the topic, my method of argument is to rely on anecdotal examples. Even a single case can at least indicate the possibility of some facet of the human experience or cultural understanding. The reader will find little in these pages regarding the results of formal surveys or statistical analyses, exceedingly few of which are highly useful given that the subject matter is found in all the world's cultures and languages. Those who must base their recognition of truth on numbers will not be happy with this study.

Finally in these regards, ethnohermeneutics demands analyses that are as free from cultural biases as is consciously possible. Hence, in these studies I posit no reality beyond the experience analyzed itself, an experience understood to be a human one. In the comparative analysis of cultural interpretations, a variety of theological and nontheological understandings will be discussed. None will be considered more valid than any other, as no culture will be considered superior to any other. For those who insist that only a particular culture's truth, their own, is valid, again, this is not a book that will please you.

This work is designed for those who wish to gain an understanding of ecstatic religious experiences, particularly the mystic experience, in a variety of cultural traditions and the many ways in which they are understood. Moreover, this work does not go beyond such understandings. Unlike many popular books on ecstatic religious experiences, this is not a work of fiction.

2

Phenomenology of the Mystic Experience

The most common publications on the mystic experience are anthologies of selections from the mystical literature. There are a number of good compilations available, as well as thematic works that incorporate excerpts from the writings of well-known mystics. Perhaps the work that raised the greatest general interest was Aldous Huxley's 1946 thematic presentation, *The Perennial Philosophy*, which influenced a generation of intellectuals, including myself. While these available self-reports by mystics are extremely important and interesting, they have been subject to reconsideration, considerable self-interpretation, and in published form, editing, and often, translation. Of more importance for ascertaining whether or not there is indeed a human, rather than cultural, common experience are self-reports unmediated by the above mentioned processes.

NAIVE REPORTS

Over the course of years, a number of students have discussed with me their own ecstatic experience. It was from these discussions that I came to realize that these experiences are not as uncommon as many religious traditions would have us understand. But, of course, I did not make a record of these conversations, as they were given spontaneously, as well as in the greatest confidence.

In England, however, there exists a unique repository of religious experiences that was crucial to this study. In the late 1960s, Sir Alister Hardy, a renowned zoologist, repeatedly made calls for individuals to send in reports of their religious experiences for research purposes. Initially, in a two year period, from 1969 to 1971, three thousand reports were gathered. Eventually this has grown to over six thousand in the archives of the Religious Experience Research Centre (RERC), presently housed at the University of Wales in Lampeter. Under the former directorship of Peggy Morgan and the superb work of Diana Hasting, this vast archive has been entered into a computerized, full-text database that makes this important resource readily available for many types of research.

At the time I worked on the files, approximately half of the material had been processed. I limited my in-depth research to these three thousand, and but rapidly perused the later thousands. Of particular importance was the earliest collection, as this was collected just prior to the New Age movement, as well as published reports based on the these archives. Hence, they are less contaminated by expectations of experience. In these files, I found ten clear cases of the mystic experience, as well as a number that were either probable or possible. The latter were so described that essential elements were not mentioned, although they may actually have been part of the experiences.

Let us begin with several of the reports of the mystic experience from the briefest descriptions to the more complex (quoted with permission of the former director). The number at the end of the quotation refers to the file number in the archive. Spelling has been corrected, but nothing else has been altered; parenthetical statements are original; brackets indicate editorial additions.

A self-description from an American woman writing of an experience sixteen years in the past:

> Inward light (not the physical spectrum from our physics) was like normal consciousness expanded to the Y [n^{th}?] degree. Personal ego vanished. Sin was not manifest. Quietness, peace, understanding, comprehension—all were as magma of light. Isolation (separate ego manifestations) were not. Physical death was not and held nothing real. Now, once back to normal consciousness I was at first deeply shook & frightened. (1066)

From an English woman in her late seventies, writing of an experience sixty years in the past:

> A certain event had hurt and humiliated me. I rushed to my room in a state of despair feeling as worthless as an empty shell.

From this point of utter emptiness it seemed as though I were caught up into another dimension. My separate self ceased to exist and for a fraction of time I seemed part of a timeless immensity of power and joy and light, something beyond this domain of life & death. My subjective and painful feelings vanished. The intensity of the vision faded, but it has remained as a vivid memory ever since. (1146)

From an English woman reporting on an experience that occurred a year before it was sent to Hardy:

A year ago while going about my normal duties as a housewife, I paused for a moment to see whether my mind was free from all thought about something which has caused me a great deal of unhappiness and pain. My mind was perfectly controlled, and I was just about to give myself a pat on the back and a well-done old girl—when! my vision was completely blacked out and light seemed all about my head—not the daylight—but a light in my mind and around—I could as it were feel the walls of my head crumbling down. I cannot explain the degree of light, there is nothing to compare it with. I seemed to become this light and consciousness of my personal self seemed to be held very faintly and of no consequence—how this light was left behind or how I came out of it I do not know, but there was another light—different—a nothing or void—which I gazed at, or was aware of. There seemed to be nothing in this second light—no body—no sound—empty—and yet I knew it wasn't empty. As quickly as I had merged into light so I once more was returned to my duties. When I say I returned of course I know that I didn't go anywhere—all I knew was that the consciousness was held by some immense power, which made my poor little effort of stout control as nothing. (613)

From a British woman who wrote of several experiences including this event thirty years in the past:

One day I had an experience which I did not understand, and will never forget. After lunch I sat at my husband's desk, & saw that he had been doodling on the blotter a tangled mess! I thought it

expressed all the difficulties he was experiencing. Can you imagine, the doodling <u>moved</u>, and formed the word "escape"! this was
astonishing enough but then "Escape" became an eye, a living lu-
minous eye, which expanded. It was magnetic. It became more
and more brilliant as it became larger, until there was nothing but
the most unimaginably brilliant living white light, expanded to
infinity. I was absorbed into this. You may not be able to believe
or understand—I don't understand it myself, because it is a unique
experience, which I can't share with anyone I have met, but I
know with the same <u>knowing</u> I have described before [she earlier
in the letter describes other experiences], that I was absorbed into
this wonderful living light, and at this moment I felt the greatest
emotion of joy I have ever felt in my life. I lost my physical self
and became one with this extraordinary expanding universe of
light. I felt very strong and thrilling vibrations that seemed to have
no beginning or end but I seemed to stretch out to infinity. Suddenly a shock, which felt like all my physical atoms coming together to form me again, and I was back in this world again. I felt
uplifted, rejuvenated, and comforted. How can I ever forget this
wonderful experience. I <u>know</u> it. (1277)

All of these experiences describe loss of self on merging into "light."
The experience was so profound that it was clearly remembered for up to six
decades. It was variously described as bliss and/or death becoming meaningless. But in all of these examples, the person seemed to have been still. Until
I received the following self-report, I had assumed that one could not be
moving during the experience since there was no awareness of self, let alone
body. A student of mine, however, had the experience while dancing in a
ballet performance. An amateur video happened to have been made of the
performance, which I have viewed. I am a ballet fan and familiar with a
number of styles and companies, but the choreography and music of this
performance were exceptionally beautiful and moving. From the video,
there is no indication that this ballerina was having any unusual experience
or an experience different from the rest of the ballet corps. I present excerpts
from her description, including the surrounding circumstances, which is the
most detailed and important I have come across, with her permission:

It is now the day of opening night. We have been rehearsing
since 10 AM. . . . There is no confusion about the pieces we are

about to perform. All the steps were finalized and any questions laid to rest more than a month ago. Since then, we have been drilling the dances over and over, making the steps our own, filling them with our life energy. We know and understand these pieces inside and out. . . . We could perform these in our sleep, and in fact, often do. Awake or asleep, all our activities seem to be performance oriented. As a group our energies are fused. We have been dancing with each other for years. . . .

Now it is our turn. We all hold hands and breathe together in unison. With eyes closed we centre ourselves, focusing our concentration directly on the present. . . . One deep breath and then it begins. . . . Within every moment of this dance is a piece of me. I am dancing Laita and Laita is dancing me. I enter the stage, embraced by the energy of the dance washing across the space. It moves through me and carries me, becoming more and more intense as the pace of the piece continues to speed up. My body is moving without instruction, for the movements are so ingrained they are known on a cellular level. This frees me to become one with the dance. . . . An overwhelming sense of joy engulfs my body. It begins at my centre and spreads upward, downward, forward, and backward until every last molecule of my self is saturated. . . . Time has stopped functioning in its normal fashion. This moment now feels like the past and the future, all at the same time. It stretches and warps, wrapping itself around me. I am so caught up in these phenomenal sensations that everything else begins to lose its vibrancy and importance to me. This world begins to disappear. First to go is my awareness of the audience, then the space I am in, the stage, the wings, the floor, and then even my fellow dancers grow dimmer until nothing more can be seen of them. But this doesn't concern me in the least; all that is left is myself moving, whirling, twirling, jumping, spinning, turning, dancing with all of my heart and soul like never before. And then a great light came to my attention. I went to it and it came to me. It grew larger, whiter, more intense. It came from everywhere, including inside of me. It moved through me and moved with me, enveloping my entire being. And then there was nothing. . . .

I hear something. I recognize it as a familiar sound but can't quite place it. Slowly the world around me starts coming into focus. I can feel my feet on the floor and am aware of my body moving. I begin to realize the space around me. I am on stage, finishing a bow. I turn and exit with the other dancers. As the applause dies off I realize that was the mystery noise I first heard. I feel great; I feel wonderful.

I haven't given this experience much thought, until now. I simply accepted the moment and instinctively locked it away in my own personal space. I didn't want to try to analyze or cate-gorize what had happened. I felt the experience was quite a nat-ural one, but also felt no need to discuss it with anyone. And even now to put this experience into a set of terms seems to trivialize it. . . . And how can I truly express with such few and menial words the vastness of it all. . . . The language limits me, for I cannot find the words to describe my existence. . . .

Her experience required a change in my understanding. It seems a highly routinized physical task, even if requiring complex movements in re-lation to music and others, will allow for the mystic experience. The dance had been rehearsed many, many times. It had become part of her being, and she could do it well, even if not present. Her experience went far in allow-ing me to understand moving meditations in relation to the mystic experi-ence; for example, the dancing of Sufi dervishes, to which we will return when discussing Islam.

Of the ten clear cases of the mystic experience found on examining the first three thousand self-reports of the RERC archives, nine were from females. The submission by a male was a small publication that contained a description of his experience, and published material is being avoided in this section. If my memory serves correctly, all of the students over the past two decades who spoke to me of their mystic experiences were females. In my study of female spirituality, *Through the Earth Darkly: Female Spiritual-ity in Comparative Perspective*, I reported the viewpoints of Chinese, Native North American, and African-Brazilian ecstatic religious functionaries that it was far easier for females to go into a trance than males because females are inherently more empathetic. Certainly, throughout the world, where women are allowed public ritual functions, far more mediums are female than male. Modern DNA research has suggested that there may well be a gene that females inherit from their fathers, in whom it is not functional, that enhances empathy. Does this empathy extend to existence as a whole? It hardly seems likely that this considerable preponderance of female reports is coincidental. In this regard, the majority of published material that focuses on male mystics may indicate cultural and institutional androcentric biases rather than the human actuality.

Two of the reports in the RERC archives involve memories from childhood. Given that young children's memories will not necessarily focus on definitive details, they may well record the mystic experience at an early age. To preface these reports, I will present my own childhood memory.

I have an extremely clear memory from the age of four—the age itself was consciously kept in the active memory from that time: I am leaning against a jeep parked at the curb in front of the apartment building in which I lived—automobiles were a rarity during World War II due to gasoline and tire rationing, and always aroused the interest of male children. I am looking up at the building and silently asking, "What am I?" Something of which I have no memory save it being inexplicable happened just prior to my questioning, while I was in the same position in the same place. This is the sharpest memory of my entire childhood.

Now why would a child of four question the nature and meaning of one's own existence? Why would the moment be burned into the memory? Why would one's age at the time it happened be a major part of that memory? I can but assume that I had the mystic experience and my memory was on coming out of it and wondering about existence itself. Here are two further related reports.

A British woman reporting on her experience more than forty years in the past when between the ages of five and eight:

> It is beyond description—I have often tried but found it very difficult:—I suddenly became aware of a tremendous beating and rhythm within my body. I can remember saying (though I felt like shouting) "I" ME—who am I? and touching my body, the flesh on my arms & legs as if asking myself what it was that made me "tick"—the feeling was overwhelming—I felt great and powerful, a part of something greater than myself. That is all I can say. (1458)

A woman brought up in England reporting on an experience that took place between the ages of eight and ten:

> I was in the garden, muddling about alone. A cuckoo flew over, calling. Suddenly, I experienced a sensation that I can

only describe as an effect that might follow the rotating of a kaleidoscope. It was a feeling of timelessness, not only that time stood still, that duration has ceased, but that I was myself out of time altogether. Somehow I knew that I was part of eternity. And there was also a feeling of spacelessness. I lost all awareness of my surroundings. With this detachment I felt the intensest joy I had ever known. . . . (1263)

My own experience led me to the assumption that one could reject the experience just prior to it becoming total, to losing one's self. Two reports in the RERC confirm that original assumption. An American male living in Georgia reports on an experience seven years in the past:

I was lying on the couch, thinking of nothing, when the lights began to fuse into one (my eyes were closed but I saw millions of little lights in my head). The lights fused into one and all but crowded that darkness out of my vision. Because of the first such experience I had some idea of what was happening, and started to control it. As soon as I tried to think the darkness seemed to start taking over my vision. I stopped trying to think and the light hesitated, came towards me, stopped, wavered, came on, completely obliterating the darkness, then it exploded into me. Not around me or over me, but into me. For the barest fraction of a moment I was overwhelmed by the sheer ecstasy of it, smothered. I couldn't stand it and purposely broke the spell . . . I came out of it almost as soon as I went into it because I couldn't stand what it was—not that it was painful, (not as we think of pain) but because Joy?! I did not hear any voices, didn't hear, feel, or see anything. I WAS. After arising I didn't feel any more moral, or better, or anything else I've been led to expect. I was shaken. . . . I have never felt, or heard of anyone else feeling what I felt, and it wasn't a feeling. It was a becoming—a being. I became absolutely nothing. Everything was nothing. (2636)

An American woman living in California reports on an experience thirty-five years in the past, when she was a student at Indiana University:

I had decided that I would stay in the church overnight, just to be doing it [staying in the church overnight]. I went to one of the social rooms where there was a couch and settled myself, hearing the preacher leave for home and knowing the church was now empty. After a bit as I sat, it was just beginning to lose some of the light, but the room was still very light, I began to observe without seeing anything and hear without actually hearing anything, a circular movement start in the upper right hand corner of the room. This movement grew gradually louder and with it a roar (not audible). There was tremendous feeling of an impersonal power entering the room, a power that belonged here and was oblivious to me. By the time the movement had reached halfway across the room and the roar had gathered a power to go with it, I was so frightened I realized that this was God coming, and nothing could stand in His way, and that I was utterly unprepared to meet Him and utterly unworthy and if I stayed I would likely lose my mind, and I got up and ran out of the church. (12)

The last report, on the whole, would not appear to be the onset of the mystic experience, save for two important factors: the circular movement and the feeling that she would lose her mind (self?) if she allowed the experience to overwhelm her. The theistic understanding expressed is not exceptional; it is found in many of the reports of experiences by devout Christians. What is exceptional, however, is the sound experience rather than or alongside (the description is not clear) of light.

A number of the self-reports in the RERC archives are probably of the mystic experience, but while loss of self is indicated, it is not clearly stated. Since it is not possible to question the respondents, particularly since these reports are over thirty years old, they are highly suggestive but remain uncertain.

An Irish-American woman living in England most of her life describes an experience sixteen years in the past, when she was twenty-one:

Still discussing and questioning [she had rejected her strict Catholic background and "swung to atheism," but still retained an interest in religion] walking alone, stood on cliff edge thinking and suddenly it happened. From green cliffs, sun, sea, sounds to a sort of suspension of time and place in which I felt most positively everything is alright, it is unity. I wasn't thinking. I wasn't seeing or physically feeling. Rather it was an awareness and oddly I felt, I'm not sure whether then or later, that I was no longer on the cliff but projected out into a grey no time which was a fullness of being. I was part of <u>it</u>. . . . All I knew at the time, and knew as I have never known before or since was unity. It wasn't me being aware I knew something. It was me being "knowing" is slightly ambiguous. I neither knew about nor knew that something was the case. By "know" I mean I experienced directly the unity. Afterwards I felt fantastically marvelous. I felt like shouting out, it's alright, no need to worry, everything is fine. (1441)

A woman who lives in India reports on an experience twenty-eight years in the past, when she was thirty-four:

<u>Immediately</u>, all physical view was blotted out and I was out of my body in a vast beam of light, seemingly OVER the mountains, and I experienced a sense of Complete and Perfect Bliss and Ecstasy. . . . I have never before nor ever since been so happy in my life and it seemed as if I were in "Perfect Being and Unity" with the whole of the Universe and Something Other indescribably exquisite. All bodily consciousness was entirely lost. (514)

An English woman, a self-declared atheist, writes of an experience twenty years in the past when she was in her mid-twenties:

It was as though my mind broke bounds and went on expanding until it merged with the Universe. Mind and universe became <u>one within the other</u>. Time ceased to exist. It was all one thing and in a state of infinity. It was as if, willy-nilly, I became directly exposed to an entity within myself and nature at large. I seemed to be "seeing" with another sight in another world. This event left an impressive afterglow which lasted many days but eventually, it faded away as mysteriously as it had come. The familiar world returned. (1481)

The last of these probable reports that will be presented is by an English woman who had the experience when she was fifteen:

Then there was complete silence except for the twittering of the birds outside in the garden; suddenly through the top of my head came a terrific heat and brilliant light which began to suffuse me, creeping down my arms and body right through my legs to my feet, tears began to come down my cheeks, and I thought to get a handkerchief but did not move. It is beyond me to describe the feelings experienced of peace joy and upliftment, I can only describe it as ecstasy, it seemed that I had become this joy and peace. (159)

If the last description is of the mystic experience, it is unusual in that occurred during a guided meditation with a hundred and fifty other people present. I have not come across any other description of the mystic experience that took place during meditation.

Finally, to conclude this presentation of naive reports, several experiences similar to the mystic experience will be presented. This will relate to the next chapter, on the varieties of religious ecstatic experiences, in order to place the mystic experience within the larger context of ecstatic experiences.

The first is of a merging-with-light experience but with no loss of the self. A sixty-seven-year old English woman reports the following experience:

It was in the spring this year [the report was sent in 1988] I was resting on our settee with my legs up. I can't recall if I was praying, but I think not, certainly I was aware. The window is across the room and gently this glorious light built up in front of the window growing ever brighter and larger until I was enveloped within it and felt myself raised up into it. At the same time there was what I can only describe as a "noiseless noise"—very beautiful. I knew it was heavenly and I was filled with delight and awe, no fear. I tried to see the face of Jesus, because I felt it was of him, but could not. I was lowered down and the light withdrew as it had come. (4921)

The following is also a merging-with-light experience but it led to an out-of-body experience. The report was sent by an English woman of an experience thirty years in the past, when she was twenty:

I was at a concert with a friend, given by the Hallé orchestra. They were playing the Chorale Symphony (Beethoven) and as I did not know the music well, I retreated into my own thoughts—which were pretty depressing. I prayed to be taken out of the "black pit of my own mind and selfishness" and suddenly, in

answer, there was a rush of LIGHT, which surrounded me, lifted
me <u>into</u> LIGHT and at the same time seemed to melt my physical
being so that LIGHT welled up also from within me, or rather,
burst out of me, to meet the LIGHT that was without. With this
LIGHT came BLISS, <u>happiness a million times stronger</u> than anything I had ever experienced on earth: and on earth I had been,
at times, completely happy. At the same time, I felt a cool
breeze playing on me, and within me a whirling sensation and a
feeling that I was somehow above myself—my body—but not
completely, only a foot or so. (1916)

For those familiar with Buddhism, particularly Mādhyamika Yogācāra,
the following experience seems related to that of the *buddhacitta* (Buddha
mind/thought). The report was written by an English male of an experience
over thirty years in the past:

. . . I became aware, as I was reading the *Manchester Guardian* as it
then was, of a most vivid sensation of entering into the mind and
consciousness of a great intelligence. At first I seemed merely to
be in contact with a mind far superior to man's and an instant
later to be part of it, and finally I realized I actually <u>was</u> that mind.
At first I observed it as something beyond and outside myself,
then of union and fusion with it, of merging and becoming it,
and finally identifying myself with it. I found myself saying:
"Why it is myself! I <u>am</u> that!" . . . It occurred in a flash of illumination, perhaps a matter of a few seconds or at most a minute or
two, but in that short period I had the feeling of knowing far
more than any lifetime of extensive and concentrated study could
give. (78)

Finally, I came across the expression of an experience that is remarkably
similar to a fourth-century Chinese poem that many sinologists consider the
perfect expression of an ineffable experience. The following was sent in by
an English woman beautifully describing an aesthetic-ecstatic experience of
nature that took place forty years in the past, when she was in her twenties:

. . . then I glanced up at the window, & a breathtaking sight met
my eyes. Framed against the blue sky was the most beautiful &
perfect pink Apple Blossom, & in a moment perhaps for a second

or two I was transported, it was as if an illuminating flash of Light?
had seared through me, I seemed to see the answer to everything,
I seemed to see God, & yet now I cannot recall what I really saw
or what the answer was, it was all over in a flash. (2592)

The poem to which I am referring is by Tao Qien (also known as Tao
Yüanming: 365-427 CE) and is the fifth poem in a series entitled, "Twenty
Poems After Drinking Wine." A translation can be found in chapter 5.

REPORTS BY "PROFESSIONAL" MYSTICS

The reports of the mystic experience found in most anthologies are from texts
that focus not so much on the experience as the interpretation of the experience. In many such reports the actual mention of the experience per se tends
to be brief, as well as obscure or oblique. This is particularly the case with reports from the monotheistic traditions, especially Christianity, as ultimate
union or utter dissolution can be understood to be heretical. Because these
reports tend to be from theologians or philosophers, I have labeled them as
reports from "professional" mystics in order to distinguish these reports from
the preceding ones I have termed "naive." This terminology is not meant to
imply that these writings are necessarily from persons making their living
based on their experience. Since virtually all of the previous reports are from
those within Christian culture, we will begin with the Religions of the Book
(Judaism, Christianity, Islam) and the influences on these traditions.

One of the clearest Christian accounts is found in the writings of
Saint Symeon (949–1022) of the Byzantine world. Other excerpts from his
writings can be found in chapter 6:

Again the light illumines me, again it is seen clearly, again it
opens the heavens, again it destroys the night, again it makes all
things disappear. Once more it alone is seen, once more it makes
me leave all the visible realities and likewise, Oh marvel! removes
me from the sensible. (Krivocheine 228)

Here we have a passage that speaks of personal experience linking the
"light" with the extinction of everything, including self, and bliss.

The Catholic theologian, Meister Eckhart (1260–c.1368), suffered a
different fate than that of Symeon. Rather than being declared a saint, he

was indicted for heresy and probably would have been convicted had he not
died before the trial. We will return to the reasons when we discuss Christian attitudes toward the experience in chapter 6. His descriptions are so explicit that the Protestant theologian Rudolph Otto (*Mysticism East and West*)
found them the easiest to compare with Hindu philosophy. Other excerpts
from Eckhart's sermons will be found in chapter 6:

> Comes then the soul into the unmixed light of God. It is trans-
> ported so far from creaturehood into nothingness . . . losing its
> own identity in the process. (Blakney 159—"unmixed" is the lit-
> eral translation)

> When the soul comes to know the real truth by that simple
> agent through which one knows God, then the soul is called a
> light. God, too, is light and when the divine light pours into the
> soul, the soul is united with God, as light blends with light.
> (Blakney 163)

> Further, I say that if the soul is to know God, it must forget itself
> and lose itself, for as long as it is self-aware and self-conscious, it
> will not see or be conscious of God. (Blakney 131)

Here we have language that is far more than theological, as it literally describes the experience of light and self-loss. It is most interesting, as we
shall see, that he also describes the experience in terms of forgetting and
losing oneself that are identical with the Chinese terminology to label the
experience to be found later in this chapter.

Around the same time as these Christian mystics, Jewish Kabbalists
were also hinting at the mystic experience. I use the word hinting, because
Kabbalism is so esoteric in both practice and imagery it is difficult to find
descriptions of actual experiences in straightforward language. Isaac of Acre
in his *Ôzar Hayyim* describes the light experience without loss of self not
uncommon in the archives of the RERC. But he also writes of union using
a common image of water, as found for example in the Upanishads, that
Moshe Idel considers "seems to have originated in personal experience":

> . . . cleaves to the Divine Intellect, and It will cleave to her, for
> more than the calf wishes to suck, the cow wishes to give suck,
> and she and the intellect become one entity, as if somebody

pours out a jug of water into a running well, that all becomes one. And this is the secret meaning of the saying of our sages: "Enoch is Metatron." (cited in Idel, *The Mystical* 128)

With regard to Islam, there are statements in the Qur'an that suggest the experience, but most of the more explicit statements are within the Sufi traditions. As with Chinese mystics, Sufi mystics tend to utilize poetry to express the mystic experience. We shall return to both of these aspects in chapter 6 with the discussion of Islam and the mystic experience. However, some of the early Sufi mystics wrote more straightforward descriptions.

Abū l-Qāsim al-Junayd, who lived a thousand years ago in Baghdad, linked bliss with self-annihilation:

> . . . the real annihilates anything to which it appears, and when it subjugates, it is first in subjugating and most real in overcoming and overpowering. . . . [The real] has subjugated them, effaced them, annihilated them from their own attributes, so that it is the real that works through them, on them, and for them in everything they experience. . . . They find bliss hidden in it, through enjoyment of existence in the mode of non-existence, insofar as the real has taken exclusive possession and complete subjugation. (Sells, *Early* 261–62)

I cannot imagine that Junayd could have written that based on solely theological speculation; it smacks of self-description.

Abd al-Karīm ibn Hawāzin al-Qushayri, who lived a century after Junayd, writes of effacement and union:

> For anyone grounded in the real, none of this is difficult. When effacement comes to dominate a person, however, he has no knowledge, no reason, no understanding, and no sense. (Sells, *Early* 115)

> But if he is snatched from all regard of creation, uprooted from his own self, utterly removed from perceiving any "other" through the sovereign power of reality when it appears and seizes him, that is union of union. . . . Union of union is the utter perishing and passing away of all perception of any other-than-God, Most Glorious and Sublime, through the onslaughts of reality. (Sells, *Early* 118)

To say that it is not difficult, I assume, could only be said by one who understands experientially.*

Let us now move on to India. As will be discussed in chapter 5, while
Buddhism is the single major religion that arises from the mystic experience, it takes ineffability to its ultimate end. Hence, the experience is never
described, following a tradition begun by Gautama Buddha himself. However, as in later Hindu philosophy, existence in and of itself is described as
ultimately empty, as is nonexistence. The Upanishads, however, contain
many references to the experience, but all oblique, and there is an enormous Hindu literature related to the experience. But direct self-descriptions
are more obscure. Let us take two contemporary examples.

Although as discussed in the preceding section of this chapter, it seems
that women are far more likely to have the experience than men, all of the
"professional" accounts so far have been by males. This most likely relates to
the androcentrism of the traditions discussed rather than proportional occurrence. In India there are exceedingly few female gurus, but there are exceptions. Charles White interviewed Satguru Swami Shri Jnanananda Saraswati
of Madras several times over a period of years in the 1970s. He writes:

> She said that she had experienced this deep absorption many
> times ever since she was a child. She added that when one is fi-
> nally fixed in it, there is no more ego. Now that absorption is al-
> ways the background of her consciousness. *Samadhi* is an
> experience without content and yet is not empty. It is complete
> fullness. "In that state I used to ask myself, 'Where am I?' . . . In
> short, it is a feeling of being simultaneously everywhere. But
> there is no perception of the physical world. The physical world
> is dissolved in the unity." (White 18)

It is difficult to culturally categorize the late Agehananda Bharati, who
will figure in a major way in the section on anthropology in chapter 4. He
is an Austrian, who in late adolescence went to India, where he was initiated into the Hindu tantric tradition and eventually became recognized in
India not only as a Hindu, one of the very few not born into the tradition,
but as a guru. He then went to the United States where he studied anthropology and became one of the founders of the Society for the Scientific
Study of Religion. He was the first Western scholar to admit to actually
having had the mystic experience and was the stimulus for my own admis-
sion. Since he identifies himself as a Hindu, and is so recognized in India, I

will so categorize him for this particular purpose. It is he who coined the term "zero-experience" to refer to the mystic experience.

Bharati relates four personal experiences he had prior to the time he wrote a book on the subject in the mid-1970s; unfortunately, none are described in detail:

> One night when I was about twelve, it happened for the first time. I was falling asleep, when the whole world turned into one: one entity, one indivisible certainty. . . . For a fraction of a minute perhaps, I saw nothing, felt nothing, but was that oneness, empty of content and feeling. (Bharati, *Light* 39)

On regaining awareness, he immediately related it to the Upanishads, which he had been reading.

His other experiences, following his practices in India, are even more briefly described, since he considers them all to be the same experience, save they were far more euphoric. One tangential point Bharati makes, however, is worth noting:

> I do not hanker after the experience—it is non-addictive for me. This lack of yearning must be a personal trait, and is not directly connected with training or affiliation. There are and were many Hindu mystics, who got highly upset about prolonged non-occurrence. . . . (Bharati, Light 46)

From my studies, however, I think his attitude is the norm, and it is primarily the professional mystics who suffer "the dark night of the soul"— the absence of the experience—and who devote their lives and activities to attempts to repeat the experience. Since the *Zhuangzi* (see following text), Bharati and myself, among many others, consider the experience unpredictable and impossible to "make happen," perhaps his attitude is the more realistic and, hence, healthier one.

As with Sufi mystics, in China the tendency was to express the ineffable experience via aesthetics, both through poetry and brushwork. The earliest extant descriptions, however, are the most explicit to be found in any early literature. They are found in the *Zhuangzi*, the earliest strata of which, probably written by a person named Zhuang Zhou, was written twenty-four centuries ago and focuses on the mystic experience. In these texts we find lucid terms to stand for the mystic experience (all translations are my own),

In the second chapter of the *Zhuangzi*, we find the brief statement: "Therefore, it is said, the Perfect Man is without self (*wuji*) . . ." (followed by two other characteristics). This chapter also has a relevant anecdote that begins with a passage describing a person in a trance state:

> Nanguo Zichi sat leaning on his armrest, looking up at the sky and breathing serenely, as though his self had lost its facade. [His disciple on asking what was happening received the reply:] "Just now, I had lost myself (*wu sang wo*). . . ."

A related term is "sitting in forgetfulness" (*zuo wang*), explained in the following:

> I allow my limbs and body to fall away, expel my intellectual faculties, leave my substance (*xing*), get rid of knowledge and become identical with the Great Universality (*da tung*); this is sitting in forgetfulness.

CONCLUSIONS

We will return to the above excerpts, with more examples and further discussion, in chapters 5 and 6. But the descriptions presented above, although limited, should be sufficient to indicate that the mystic experience is a human experience. It is an experience that cannot be predicted and work toward causing the experience may be fruitless. It is an experience that is unforgettable and may effect one's understanding ever afterward. Because it is contentless, it can be interpreted in a number of ways and found to verify contradictory theological and philosophical positions.

My personal preference is for the descriptive terminology found in the earliest strata of the *Zhuangzi*, as it is free of any culturally bound theological or philosophical position. These terms include, "losing one's self" or "self-loss" (in the sense of utter disappearance of self), and "sitting in forgetfulness" (of self and everything else). These terms are compatible with Bharati's "zero-experience" and "null-experience" used by some contemporary psychologists.

Being ineffable, there is considerable reluctance by many who have had the experience to discuss it for any number of reasons. For those lacking a theological grounding, there may be fear that others would think one insane. And for those with such grounding, there may be fear of being accused of blasphemy, if not heresy. Or the experience may be so powerful and yet so private that there is a reluctance to share it for concern of its being trivialized. Of the three thousand files examined in the RERC, the number of reports of the mystic experience is exceedingly small. But this may not indicate that very few have it. It is possible that other ecstatic experiences, such as visions, not being ineffable, lend themselves to being discussed with others. The majority of those who have the mystic experience, for any number of reasons beyond the ones suggested, may simply not wish to discuss or describe it. Again the proportionally small number of such descriptions among acknowledged mystics of the Religions of the Book may also indicate that mystics of these traditions are more comfortable discussing visions and other ecstatic experiences rather than the mystic experience. In other traditions, such as shamanistic and mediumistic ones, the mystic experience, being nonfunctional, may not seem to be as important as those central to one's functioning and sociocultural needs.

In the next chapter, we shall examine the varieties of ecstatic religious experiences in order to place the mystic experience within the diverse array of ecstatic experiences. This will assist in understanding the unique character of the mystic experience.

3

The Varieties of
Ecstatic Experience

Reading through the thousands of self-reports contained in the Religious
Experience Research Centre's archives, described in the preceding chapter,
one encounters a panoply of ecstatic religious experiences, virtually all the
types of experiences had by those of British and related cultures in the
twentieth century. The following sketch of these experiences is but in-
tended to place the mystic experience in the context of ecstatic religious
experiences in general.

The experience of light, whether described as intense white or golden,
is a common aspect of the mystic experience but also is found in other experiences. Not infrequently, one encounters reports of the light alone, often
leading to an interpretation that affects the person's life. Or the light experience leads to a vision within the light, often for Christians a vision of Jesus. In
a very few cases, as the one quoted in the previous chapter, the light experience led to an out-of-body experience. These experiences involve a feeling
of being lifted from one's body or floating above it, which is one of the common features of near-death experiences (to be discussed later in this chapter),
but the experience also occurs in and of itself. This experience is closely related to those of traveling outside of one's body, sometimes termed "astral
projection" in contemporary culture with its science fiction substrate.

Related to but far less frequent than light experiences are those of
sound, which can be as overwhelming as the light. These tend to be understood variously as hearing God, the music of the spheres or cosmos, and so
forth. Visions are reported without, to the writers of the self-reports, other
notable features. Most commonly these visions are of angels, Christ, God,
or an unspecified numinous being.

Connected with the previously mentioned internal sensory-type experiences or often occurring separately is a feeling of intense well-being or peacefulness. For Christians, this is understood as experiencing God's love, and may arise from a profound experience of faith.

The ecstatic experience of self-loss, the mystic experience, as we have seen in the preceding chapter is often understood as a union experience as well as an experience of nothingness. Far more frequent are unitive experiences without the loss of self. In other words, we experience a union with God or the cosmos or a merging with a larger entity, but we remain aware of ourselves being so conjoined; that is, the union is not total, for we still exist, in some sense, and remain cognizant of the union.

A very common experience, particularly for those professing Christianity, are conversion experiences, of which there have been many studies. Many of the adult-baptism sects (Anabaptist), especially Pentecostalism, create an atmosphere that encourages acceptance of their religion in an experience so intense that, not infrequently, it is ecstatic.

The simplest type of conversion experience is a profound realization of the truth of the religion's message. But this intense, at times ecstatic, realization may be nontheological; it is the complete and total realization of anything one considers a profound truth. In Christian theology, this is called an "epiphany."

What causes these experiences? From the reports, there seem to be many so-called triggers. These would include near-death experiences, the effects of meditation, the experience of childbirth, the effects of intense prayer or meditation, and the use of psychotropic substances (those substances that affect the brain). Nitrous oxide ("laughing gas") was often used in dentistry in the early twentieth century to alleviate pain, and not uncommonly, led, for those so inclined, to religious experiences. An intense aesthetic experience, often of nature—a sunset, a beautiful scene, flowers, music, a painting, and so forth—may lead to a unitive experience or simply an experience so intense that it is, in itself, ecstatic. For those theologically inclined, ecstatic religious experiences are due to the grace of God.

A very different category of experience from the above are events that happen in our lives that so affect us that the recognition of the experience's import is similar to an ecstatic experience. These include experiences of healing oneself or a relative, being saved from a physical disaster or in battle, having a precognition of something happening to a member of one's family, or surviving the death of a long-term spouse. While these, in themselves, may not be ecstatic experiences, they may so affect people that they are understood as religious and so reported to the Centre.

Some of the reports of religious experience are not actually those of the persons writing the letters but descriptions of what was observed. These generally are of occult experiences, such as the use of a Ouija board or of being at a spiritualist seance.

HUMAN NATURE AND ECSTATIC EXPERIENCES

The many thousands of reports gathered over but a few years in the Religious Experience Research Centre's archives indicates that ecstatic religious experiences are far from uncommon. My own experience in teaching courses on mysticism over a couple of decades is similar; virtually all of my students have had such experiences, with a few having the mystic experience. Various sociological surveys suggest the same (see chapter 4). Andrew Weil (19) has taken this understanding a step further, arguing that the "desire to alter consciousness periodically is an innate, normal drive analogous to hunger or the sexual drive":

> In particular, the omnipresence of the phenomenon argues that we are dealing not with something socially or culturally based but rather with a biological characteristic of the species. Furthermore, the need for periods of nonordinary consciousness begins to be expressed at ages far too young for it to have much to do with social conditioning. Anyone who watches very young children without revealing his presence will find them regularly practicing techniques that induce striking changes in mental states. Three- and four-year-olds, for example, commonly whirl themselves into vertiginous stupors. They hyperventilate and have other children squeeze them around the chest until they faint. They also choke each other to produce loss of consciousness.

Ecstatic experience may even be more important than food for humans, assuming there is sufficient food for survival. For example, many anthropologists assume that horticulture began with the need to insure a steady supply of grain or tubers for the manufacture of beer, a psychoactive beverage. Beer or wine is an essential characteristic of religious rituals in most religions worldwide, the notable exceptions being Buddhism and Islam. Ritual inebriation may be expected, as, for example, in the Jewish festival of Purim. Four cups of wine are mandated in the Pesach Seder, although wine as an alcoholic beverage became more symbolic than actual in the Christian variation of the Pesach Seder ritual: the Eucharist from the Last Supper, which also borrows from Mithraic ritual. Even in secular use, the drinking of alcohol frequently involves the use of rituals found with no other beverage; the toast is ubiquitous in human cultures.

The traditional ritual use of other psychoactive substances ranges from coca in the Andes and peyote in Mesoamerica, to marijuana in India and the mushroom *Amanita muscaria* in Siberia, and the social use of coffee and tea has become worldwide. In the 1960s, chemically produced derivatives of natural psychoactive substances, such as LSD, mescaline, and psilocybin, became moderately popular among Western intellectuals as a means to induce ecstatic experiences, often understood as religious. In response, Western governments freaked out and banned all seriously psychoactive substances that they did not already heavily tax and on which they were thus financially dependent, such as alcohol and tobacco.

There are also nonsubstance means of eliciting ecstasy, such as marching. The shift of warfare from mechanically released missiles (arrows) to those shot with explosives (firearms) led to the use of massed soldiers with smoothbore muskets (unaimed) against each other, reaching its final stage in the massed charges against machine guns in World War I. The winning side was the one least decimated. This technological development (I would hardly call it an advance) led to military training becoming primarily that of marching en masse and in step, reminiscent of the development of the phalanx in early Greek warfare and continuing into the Roman period. Those who have had such training know that marching leads to a loss of individual identity and thinking to a temporary state of immersion into a group identity, which can be euphoric, similar to the ritual use of psychoactive substances, especially if appropriate music (marches) designed to enhance the psychological state is utilized. Most people, especially youths, enjoy marching and other mass activities.

The more popular contemporary equivalent to marching is loss of self in sports stadiums where many tens of thousands of individuals willingly lose themselves into a group euphoria; the equivalent takes place in "raves," rock concerts, political rallies, and so forth. This is now being recognized as both an ecstatic state and a fundamental human desire in even the popular media, such as *Time* magazine: "There is a human need . . . to achieve the ecstatic merger with the mass represented by the wave or the chop [referring to American professional football games]" (Ehrenreich 60).

Dream research begun in the 1950s and experimentation with psychoactive substances in the 1960s led to increased realization of the commonality of ecstatic and other nonordinary states of consciousness. The classic formulation for this complex of phenomena is Arnold Ludwig's (104) expression, "altered states of consciousness," or ASC, referring to

> . . . those mental states, induced by various physiological, psychological, or pharmacological maneuvers or agents, which can be recognized subjectively by the individual himself (or by an objective observer of the individual) as representing a sufficient deviation, in terms of subjective experience or psychological functioning, from certain general norms as determined by the subjective experience and psychological functioning of that individual during alert, waking consciousness.

More recently, those working in this area (e.g., Zinburg) have substituted the word "alternate" for "altered" which is more in keeping with the lessened focus on the effects of psychoactive substances. It is important to note that ASCs include dreaming.

In summary, all of us, as human beings, not only have various sorts of alternate states of consciousness, including ecstatic ones, but we seek and desire them. That these states, so important to us, are part and parcel of most religions is to be expected, in that religion encompasses that which is most important to us. Those modern religions that eschew ecstasy find their congregants dwindling or finding ecstasy outside of the nominally religious practices and in assumed secular practices, such as spectator sports. But we should keep in mind that sports, from ball games arising in indigenous American cultures, to the archery contests of early Chinese sacrificial meals, to the Olympic martial sports of Hellenic civilization, were all originally religious rituals. In any case, as REM (rapid eye movement) sleep research has proven, we all dream.

The last set of reports brings us to phenomena not reported in the letters to the Centre, at least in the initial set of three thousand, but to those experiences for which there is vast, expanding literature, experiences that are often the focus of New Age religion. These are the functional religious ecstacies and ecstatics of shamanism, mediumism, and prophecy.

FUNCTIONAL ECSTASIES

In all cultures, save the monotheistic ones, certain types of ecstatic religious behavior are socially significant and may also have important functions. These experiences may be the means for others to directly experience the numinous, be crucial for subsistence, be important to healing in the larger sense, be central to leadership of many types, be the primary means for individuals to make decisions or function for others, and so forth.

Visions, Lucid Dreams, and Problem-Solving Dreams

Ubiquitous in all cultures are visions or the auditory equivalent, that is, hearing voices. In contemporary Western culture, these experiences, especially the latter, are considered a symptom of schizophrenia. Often there is no distinguishing by psychiatrists between hearing voices as a negative experience—constant, disturbing, driving individuals to commit acts that are socially disapproved—or a positive one that enhances the life of the individual or society. By labeling these experiences hallucinations, a value judgment is placed on the experience of others; that is, if the person making the judgment has not had the same experience as another, the other's experience cannot be real or valid. In effect, this attitude would deny the validity of the Religions of the Book, since the Hebrew Bible is largely understood to be based on individuals hearing revelations from the Divine; the New Testament is, in part, based on visions reported by the Apostles; and the Qu'ran arises from the revelations to Muhammad. As is evident from the religious literature and the Religious Experience Research Centre's archives, visions are relatively common and usually benign, if not propitious.

Similar to visions, or, at least so they are understood in many cultures, are lucid dreams. One common definition of lucid dreams are dreams in which one seems to be aware that one is dreaming. I prefer the definition that lucid dreams are those we not only remember but perceive as very meaningful; this fits the many cultures that do not distinguish between these types of dreams and visions while awake. Lucid dreaming, which, I assume, we all have experienced at some time in our lives, is perhaps the most commonly reported ecstatic experience.

In all cultures, prior to modern Western culture, it was understood that we all dreamed, and dreaming was an important activity. Freud popularized the notion that the primary if not sole value of dreams is to diagnose and delineate neuroses, suggesting that a mentally healthy person would not dream. Later dream research shattered these modern Western notions and brought us closer to the more common cultural understanding of dreaming. One major use of dreams in pre-modern cultures is problem-solving. Conscious, rational thinking is but one of the many ways humans work out problems, and it is not always the most effective one.

Most, if not all, scientific breakthroughs are the result of inspiration, that is, of unconscious reasoning processes—dreams, whether awake (daydreams or reveries) or asleep. How many of us have awoken with a solution to a problem that had been bothering us or a solution to a seemingly insoluble problem. When I was studying literary Chinese in my early twenties, I invariably encountered one or more passages I could not translate. I developed a technique of using dreaming to solve them. I would place a lamp, a pad with a list of difficult passages, and a pen by my side of the bed. Before going to sleep, I would look at an insoluble passage, then turn off the light. Invariably, I would awaken with a solution, turn on the light, write it down, look at the next problem passage, turn off the light, and go back to sleep. Usually this method resolved all translation difficulties, and stood the light of day. My doctoral dissertation, a reconstruction and annotated translation of such a text, was eventually published in the prestigious T'oung Pao monograph series (*The Fu-tzu*).

A half-century of neuroscientific research has moved the scientific understanding far from the early psychoanalytic conception of dreams. The perception of dreaming in other cultures is not only accepted, but there have been a number of studies to ascertain the nature of brain activity that dreaming involves. Jonathan Winson (58), who has devoted his scientific career to the study of dreaming and memory, summarizes this approach:

> Based on recent findings in my own and other neuroscientific laboratories, I propose that dreams are indeed meaningful. Studies of the hippocampus (a brain structure crucial to memory), of rapid eye movement (REM) sleep and of a brain wave called theta rhythm [important in meditation research] suggest that dreaming reflects a pivotal aspect of the processing of memory. In particular, studies of theta rhythm in subprimate animals have provided an evolutionary clue to the meaning of dreams. They appear to be a nightly record of a basic mammalian memory process: the means by which animals form strategies for survival and evaluate current experience in light of those strategies. The

existence of this process may explain the meaning of dreams in human beings.

SHAMANISM

The concept of "shamanism" became known among European intellectuals based on Russian ethnology in Siberia and Danish ethnology among the Inuit, and was popularized, without the term, in the Noble Prize winning 1945 novel of Hermann Hesse, *Das Glasperlenspiel* (translated into English as *The Bead Game* in 1949) with an attached story called, "The Rainmaker." In 1951, the pioneering historian of religions, Mircea Eliade published his tome, *Le Chamanisme et les techniques archaïques de l'extase* (translated into English in 1964 as *Shamanism: Archaic Techniques of Ecstasy*). Eliade's method is to uncritically utilize an enormous amount of published ethnographic material of varying quality that is slotted into a series of categories. He treats shamanism as the ur-religion of the distant past, and it seems unlikely that he ever met a functioning shaman. Eliade's work, in English translation, led to the popularity of his romanticized depiction of shamans among intellectuals in North America.

A few years later, Carlos Castaneda began to publish a series of fictional works relating shamanism to psychoactive substances (in large part based, sometimes quite inaccurately, on Peter Furst's and Barbara Meyerhoff's research on the Huichol of Mexico and their ritual use of peyote to elicit trance—Castaneda was their graduate student at UCLA). Castaneda claimed these imaginary narratives to be participant-observation ethnological studies, and they were enormously influential on those seeking alternatives to traditional Western modes of religion (see de Mille).

Shortly thereafter, the anthropologist Michael Harner, who had carried out excellent ethnological studies of Amazonian traditions (e.g., *The Jivaro*) published his *Hallucinogens and Shamanism* in 1973 that, along with the research of a number of others, confirmed the relationship between psychoactive plants and shamanism. It came to be understood in the popular mind that one could ingest a particular substance and become a "shaman." Harner then moved into the realm of New Age training, publishing in 1980, *The Way of the Shaman: A Guide to Power and Healing*, which, according to the flyleaf, "is an introductory handbook of shamanic methodology for health and healing." It also served as a text for weekend workshops given around the world by himself and his disciples, in which, for a fee of several hundred dollars, one could become a "shaman." Harner's approach was not to utilize psychoactive substances but drumming and guided imagery. In any New Age bookstore, one will presently find a plethora of do-it-yourself books on shamanism, as well as journals dedicated to the subject carrying travel advertisements to countries where one my have "authentic" shamanistic experiences.

Eliade never defines "shamanism" but does consider trance-flight the defining characteristic. The term itself derives from a Tungus (northeastern Siberia—Altaic language family) word for their ritual specialists. Scandinavian scholars had long been studying the phenomena with regard to the Saami (Lapp) traditions of northern Scandinavia and elsewhere (e.g., Carl-Martin Edsman, Bäckman). Åke Hultkrantz, who achieved doctorates in both history of religions and anthropology, carried out fieldwork studies of Shoshoni religion in Wyoming. He disagrees with Eliade's understanding that trance-flight is a necessary condition of shamanism, and his definition of a "shaman" is far more precise: a shaman is "a social functionary who, with the help of guardian spirits, attains ecstasy to create a rapport with the supernatural world on behalf of his [or her] social group" ("A Definition" 34). Hultkrantz, as many scholars of shamanism, would deny there is any actual religious phenomenon called "shamanism" per se but that the term refers to a functional mode of religiosity found within particular circumpolar and Native American religious traditions. Hultkrantz has also pointed out that shamans function via varying degrees of trance, ranging from virtually comatose states to those in which the trance is so light that it would be imperceptible to all but those familiar with the particular shaman.

Nonetheless, there is a tendency to use the word "shamanism" far more broadly. British and some American scholars tend to use the term for any mode of functional ecstacy, including mediumism or spirit possession (e.g., I. M. Lewis, Kendall). Continental scholars, including Eliade, usually exclude possession trances from shamanism; for example, Gilbert Rouget (18) writes: "In my opinion shamanic trance and possession trance constitute two very different—and indeed opposite—types of relationship with the invisible. . . ." A number of books by religionists have increasingly used the term to represent spirituality in general, perhaps beginning with a book that argued that biblical prophets and ordained Catholic priests were shamans; that is, anyone considered holy. Hence, the popularity of the New Age focus.

In Siberian cultures, the shaman is a semi-specialist, neither the charismatic figure of European romanticism nor the socially accepted mentally ill figure of contemptuous Russian scholarship. In northern Native American traditions, at least prior to the forced relocation to reservations, all members of the cultures functioned shamanistically to varying degrees. The anthropologist Lowie (312) termed this "democratized shamanism." I have suggested that in gathering-hunting traditions, it was understood to be essential that all members of society had a personal relationship with one or more guardian spirits in order to both survive and carry out activities necessary to their community, and that there were means for communal trances to facilitate group action (see "'Sweat Lodge'"). Of course, as with any ability, some individuals will be better at it than others; for example, all healthy individuals can run, but some run faster than others. In other words, democratized shamanism was the original norm and only under changed religio-ecological circumstances, such as a shift from hunting to herding did individuals specialize in shamanic behavior, either due to hereditary circumstances or talent.

My own understanding is based on continuing relationships with functioning Native American shamans over several decades, as well as my own personal limited experience in this regard (based on years of intense experiences in a Native American community). The key features as I understand them follow those of Hultkrantz's aforementioned definition: (1) functioning (2) with the assistance of spirits (3) in a mild to deep trance state (4) in order to help another individual or a group. In all cultures incorporating shamanism with which I am familiar, the most evil and dangerous thing a person can do is act shamanistically for oneself or even one's own family. In the past, such a person was liable to be executed and, in the present, to be shunned. It is also commonly assumed that to act in this way would lead to injury or death of the person doing it or of a member of his or her family. Hence, New Age shamanizing, in the main, would be considered evil sorcery and, indeed, may be inherently dangerous to those who have little understanding of what they are doing.

Traveling via trance is simple. When undergraduate students were less passive than now, I assisted the students in my mysticism course (after the class ended) at their request to do so. All but one were able to go somewhere. What is more important is that one has a purpose for the journey and can act for others when there; the journey in and of itself is virtually irrelevant. Nor is it necessary to go anywhere, or if it is, one can ask a spirit to go there on one's behalf. The relationship with spirits while in a shamanistic trance is complex. One can ask the spirits to come to one, one can go to where the spirits are, one can merge with a spirit(s) while maintaining one's own will, identity. The primary difference from spirit possession in this regard is that one retains while in trance both awareness and one's own volition, even though one can do nothing without the aid of spirits, since it is their powers that allow the necessary tasks to be accomplished, not one's own.

In extant gathering-hunting traditions, or their continuations into the modern context, it is understood that all entities on which human life is dependent—animals, plants, minerals, weather phenomena—are numinous (in Hallowell's generally accepted term, "other-than-human beings"). Animals are not so much hunted as asked to sacrifice themselves out of compassion so humans may live. Simultaneously, humans need the abilities of predator animals to attain herbivores, humans' primary source of animal protein, save for maritime cultures. This would have been even more the situation several tens of thousands of years ago, when humans were hunting larger and more dangerous herbivores (megafauna) than exist today. They needed power to attain these animals, and they needed a means for working closely together for a group hunt. Shamanistic rituals satisfy both these needs. On the one hand, these rituals considerably enhance human abilities to find and attain needed food sources through the assistance of the numinous, and communal rituals that enable a group trance—sweat lodge or use of psychoactive substances—create a climate in which people can temporarily work together in close rapport. This understanding, combined with analyses of early human art remaining in caves, strongly indicates that shamanism was at the basis of very early human religious behavior.

This need not mean that shamanism is necessarily "primitive" and irrelevant to contemporary culture. The male and female shamans I know personally are Native American healers who are quite comfortable in modern culture. Most live in large cities and have advanced university degrees (MA, MTh, or PhD) yet heal in traditional ways with the help of assisting spirits, which, given the urban context, are now as likely to be dead humans (ghosts) as animals.

As an ecstatic religious experience, shamanistic trance is empowering in two interrelated ways. First, there is the rapture of intimately relating to numinous entities, whether they be theriomorphic, ghost, or other types of spirits. Second, there is the elation that follows from knowing that one has helped others.

MEDIUMISM

I define a medium as a social functionary whose body only, the person's awareness suppressed while in an ecstatic state, serves as a means for spirits to assist and/or communicate with members of the medium's group in a positive manner. Thus, undesirable possession by malevolent spirits is excluded from this definition, which in virtually all cultures, including Christianity, mandates exorcism. Moreover, the term is not necessarily germane to the "mediums" of Spiritualism that developed in mid-nineteenth-century America and Europe, since they do not usually undergo full possession trance in which the spirits appear in their bodies, but rather receive messages from the dead. Spiritualism, combined with African influences, has led to professional spiritualists who claim possession trance, and combined with Theosophy or science fiction, claim multivolume book-length messages from lost worlds (Atlantis, Mu) or outer space.

In classic spirit-possession mediumism, mediums do not remember what occurred while in trance, since only their bodies but not their minds are present. Spirits take over a person's body to directly minister to people, while the owner of the body, so to speak, is in effect away or asleep. In many cultures, it is common for a second person to interpret the words or writings of the possessed medium. The medium is incapable of such interpretation either during or after the trance, given that the medium is unaware of what has taken place. Mediums who have a frenetic trance often require assistance for their physical safety, and when the spirit leaves the possessed person, such mediums frequently collapse. They must be caught by others before they hit the ground and possibly suffer injury, since there is often a slight delay in regaining consciousness and taking back control over one's body.

Theory and actuality may not always jibe, especially when theoretical constructs fuse together. For example, shamanism and mediumism not only coexist in East Asia but may merge in some instances, particularly in Korea, where mediums may be aware of their trance experiences (see the descriptions in Kendall). In the distant past of Korea, shamanistic Altaic culture merged with the mediumistic culture of more southern, rice-cultivating East Asia.

Different from shamanism, mediumism has not been romanticized. Indeed, there is a modern Western tendency to see mediumism solely as a means for socially marginal individuals, especially women, to attain a modicum of status (see I. M. Lewis for the classic depiction) rather than being charismatic leaders as is often assumed for shamanism. Mediums are frequently perceived as ignorant, if not mentally deficient. In part, this may be due to the fact that most mediums worldwide are female, and this valuation of mediums reflects traditional Western misogyny. Moreover, modern Westerners value individualism over subordination to society and tend to dread any state that would lead to their loss of personal identity, no matter how temporary.

In actuality, mediums often have had a high status in early kingship, ranging from the earliest in Sumeria, through the early Chinese empire and the African kingdoms. Along with shamanism, mediumism preserves early human religious behavior. While shamanism seems to have been part and parcel of gathering-hunting traditions, mediumism, combined with familism, seems to be normative to horticulture-hunting traditions, save for the Americas. In the Western hemisphere, shamanism continued into horticultural and agricultural situations, but combined with elements of familism. Familism (ancestor worship) refers to the religious construct, central to the indigenous religious traditions of Africa, much of Asia and Polynesia, in which the family and the larger clan are the focus of religious rituals. The primary rituals consist of offerings of food and drink to the dead of the family, who in turn enhance the fortunes of the family. Individuals see themselves first and foremost as members of a family and clan; they serve the dead while alive, knowing that they will become spirits revered by their descendants upon their own death.

Gathering-hunting traditions tend to ritually avoid the dead. For example, some gathering-hunting traditions around the northern Great Lakes, after a year's mourning, held a final feast for the deceased and then asked the spirit of the deceased not to return. Horticulture-hunting traditions, to the contrary, revere the dead. As examples, some traditions grind up the bones of the family dead and mix them into a drink to be ingested by the living family members; others bury the bones in large communal pits. Prior to the arrival of Europeans, Iroquoian-speaking cultures around the eastern Great Lakes, when it was time to move due to depleted horticultural fields every ten to fifteen years, brought all the corpses buried in the related villages together and buried them, following elaborate ceremonies, in a large ossuary.

The reason for this difference is not difficult to understand. For gathering-hunting traditions leading a seminomadic existence in small groups, the corpse is a spiritually potent element irrelevant to their subsistence patterns, which are dependent on animal and plant spirits (who may at times appear in anthropomorphic form). Horticulture-hunting cultures tend to reside in large matrilineal/matrilocal clan dwellings organized in semipermanent villages near the clan gardens. The clan dead contribute to the strength of the clan and are buried close to the living to enhance clan continuity.

As horticulture becomes more important than hunting, theriomorphic spirits give way to anthropomorphic ones. In early agricultural societies, the transition becomes complete, and ancestral spirits take on effective roles. Incorporation of anthropomorphic spirits is different from that of theriomorphic spirits as the human spirits fit comfortably into human bodies. Moreover, there would be far more equanimity with the incorporation of a dead family member—a beloved grandmother or grandfather—than of a potentially dangerous nonhuman spirit. Such incorporation could become temporarily total, allowing the dead family elder to continue to directly advise the family. Given millennia of familiarity with spirit possession by the family dead, as other spirits become anthropomorphized, so too they can directly interrelate with the human community through trance possession.

At the earliest known settled agricultural site to date, Çatalhöyük in central Anatolia, dating to approximately 9000 BP (before present), dead adults were buried under the sleeping platforms of the homes, while children were buried under the floors. The simplest explanation is that this practice would enhance the opportunity for people to communicate with the dead in their dreams and, perhaps, to be possessed by them. Children were not needed for advice and were buried to keep them nearby but not under the beds. It is quite possible that mediumism was present in Çatalhöyük; certainly it was later omnipresent throughout the larger area.

In the earliest agricultural civilization for which we have written records regarding ritual roles, Sumeria, the "Lady Deity" (*nin-dinger*) was probably the female high priest. She was of elevated social status and would probably have been possessed by the deity Inanna (in later periods, Ishtar), who had ritual intercourse with her divine consort Dumuzi (later Tammuz), represented by or incarnated in the king. By the historical period, the "Sacred Marriage Rite" functioned as the validation of Mesopotamian kingship. In cities aside from Inanna's Uruk, the woman participating in the ritual was usually possessed by the female protector deity of the city or the consort of the city's male protector deity. Most commonly, she was identified with Inanna/Ishtar in order to associate the city's ruler with the powerful female deity (see Stuckey).

Mediumism and agriculture went hand in hand throughout the world, except possibly for the Americas. In the latter area, all the other attributes regarding the dead are found, except that shamanism seems not to have been displaced by mediumism. Our knowledge of the nature of ritual trance of the agricultural civilizations is quite limited, however, due to the Spanish destruction of the Native libraries. Nonetheless, the continuing indigenous religions of the nonelite are definitely shamanistic.

In China, until about twelve hundred years ago, in the elite clan sac-rificial rituals, a descendant of the primary recipient was possessed by him or her to enable the presence of the dead spirit at the ceremony. Until this time too, professional mediums had been officials at the imperial court and were the only females in the government. For at least the last thousand years, all of the effective nonfamily spirits were dead humans who had demonstrated their beneficence to the living and were contacted through the possession of a living member of the community. In China, which has been highly literate for millennia, spirits may communicate with the living by writing, using the body of a possessed literati. In Chinese religion, we have the unique instance of written autobiographies by deities. In the central African kingdoms, a sim-ilar pattern is found, save for the literary aspects. Spirit possession allows the living to be in direct contact with the numinous. Faith is irrelevant when people can touch and be touched by the deities and speak with them directly.

Although in China and elsewhere mediums are often uneducated, this is not an essential feature of mediumism. Among my female friends in Taiwan are highly intelligent and articulate mediums, as well as initiated Daoist priests who hold advanced university degrees and, at times, function through spirit possession. I have met literary mediums there who were university deans and bank vice presidents.

As an ecstatic experience, spirit possession offers little to the medium save for the knowledge that she or he is helping others. Mediums may be reluctant to take on the burden, but if the spirit chooses them, they have lit-tle choice. Those chosen who refuse the role sometimes find their health deteriorating and are only restored to well-being by accepting their role. (For a more thorough analysis of mediumism, both in theory and practice, see Paper, *The Spirits*, "Mediums" and *Through the Earth*.)

PROPHECY

Prophecy and prophets are part of the religious heritage in the West due to their importance in the Hebrew Bible and in Islam. Judaism understands prophecy to be limited to the biblical period, and Islam understands Muhammad to be the last prophet—to assume a later one is heresy and may be punished by execution, as has occurred in contemporary Iran. In other cultures, certain historical figures have been described as prophets in the Western literature, by which is meant that these persons brought a religious message received as a revelation to their community. While it is clear that some of the biblical prophets had visual and/or auditory visions, it is far from certain that all revelations came while in an ecstatic trance. Nor would the relationship with a monotheistic deity allow for the type of intercourse between human and deities that takes place in polytheistic traditions. Hence, to equate prophets with shamans as some scholars have done requires a considerable stretch of the concepts. While prophecy is often understood as an aspect of mysticism, it is difficult to discuss such an amorphous concept as a mode of ecstatic religious experience.

NONFUNCTIONAL ECSTASIES

In contemporary Western culture there tends to be little interest in functional ecstasies, although it is the functional ecstasies that have been of primary importance throughout the span of human history. The exception to this generalization would be the New Age interest in aspects of shamanism with the social function removed, which means it would no longer be shamanistic. Nonfunctional ecstasies do occur in shamanistic and mediumistic traditions, as will be discussed in chapters 5 and 7, but they are understood to be less important than the functional ones. There are many types of nonfunctional ecstatic experiences, and examples are provided at the beginning of this chapter. Those experiences often understood as closest to the mystic experience, if not confused with it, are frequently termed "unitive experiences."

UNITIVE EXPERIENCES

The most common type of unitive experience is probably sexual climax, in which individuals feel themselves to become one with rapture in and of itself, and, as well, may at times feel a very temporary, ecstatic union with the sexual partner. Another common type of unitive experience is the aesthetic one, in which the individual has a rapturous sensation of merging with a sunset, a beautiful scene, a piece of music, a painting, and so forth. Related are experiences of physical fulfillment, a "personal best" in athletics, attaining the peak of a difficult mountain or perfection in dance, in which there is nothing but the experience of the moment, a moment in which the experiencer feels at one with all that is perceived and the activity in and of itself.

Similarly, race car drivers, masters of many martial arts and so forth, attain a state in which they, the vehicle or weapon, and the action are a singularity. I have heard race car drivers discuss such a state, and an adage in

Japanese *kendo* (the "way of the sword") is that ideally "the mind and sword are one." For in these activities, thinking is too slow and can but lead to death or injury; there is no time for cogitation, only the action. It is only when the person is able to integrate mind and racing car or weapon so that the most efficacious action takes place without conscious thought can talent and training be maximized. These too are unitive experiences that again are euphoric.

Meditation can also lead to unitive experiences as an intermediate stage of development (see the following section on pure consciousness for a more advanced stage: consciousness-itself). Arthur Deikman ("Implications of Experimentally Induced Contemplative Meditation") experimentally induced such an experience by having subjects focus on a blue vase. He mistakenly, in "Deautomatization and the Mystic Experience," then assumed such a state of unity (with the blue vase) was identical to LSD experiences, as well as the mystic experience. More traditionally, formal meditation can lead to experiencing union with the cosmos or Godhead, depending on the ideological basis of the tradition.

Most of the mystical literature, either by mystics or by analysts of mysticism (e.g., Happold) focus on unitive experiences, especially those of union with the highest goal of various religious traditions (a complex issue in the monotheistic traditions, see chapter 6), unless the goal is the mystic experience itself (as in Buddhism and Hinduism, see chapter 5). More recent analyses (e.g., Merkur, *Mystical Moments*) understand unitive experiences to be types of experiences rather than to stand for mysticism in its entirety or its peak. In these experiences, rapturous as they may be, the experiencer, while losing her or himself in the merging, in the oneness, stills retains consciousness and a strong memory of the experience.

There is also a literature on the effects of psychedelic substances and ecstatic experiences. Most studies relate the effects of these substances with shamanistic and vision-type experiences (e.g., Furst; Harner, *Hallucinogens*), but Dan Merkur (*Ecstatic Imagination* 96–97) also relates unitive experiences to those arising from the ingestion of particular psychoactive substances, seemingly valuing substance-induced unitive and other experiences over naturally occurring (spontaneous) ones:

> As psychedelic unions occur at lower dosage levels, they are indistinguishable in almost all respects from spontaneously occurring unitive experiences. . . . Significant differences arise at the higher dosage levels, because psychedelic unions are then more powerful than spontaneously occurring ecstasies.

Merkur is here referring to the temporal length of the ecstasy, which he understands to lead to more profound and lasting effects. He also states:

> . . . mysticisms that are based on trance states are invariably irra-
> tional and generally otherworldly, whereas psychedelic unions
> leave the sense of reality intact. Although psychedelic ecstasies
> are intrinsically speculative, they are often rational and frequently
> pertain to the physical world of sense perception.

From my own experiences and those with whom I have discussed these matters who are experienced in both types of ecstasies, I must not only disagree with Merkur on these points, but would tend, in general, to reverse them, save for the duration aspect.

PURE CONSCIOUSNESS

Training in meditation can lead to an experience that has been variously termed "pure consciousness," "consciousness-itself," and "consciousness-only":

> Pure consciousness is "pure" in the sense that it is free from the
> processes and contents of knowing. It is a state of "consciousness"
> in that the knower is conscious through the experience, and can,
> afterwards, describe it. The "content" of pure consciousness is
> self-awareness. (Travis and Pearson 79)

This condition is an oft-stated achievable goal of various Hindu meditation schools, as well as Buddhism, especially Chan (Zen) Buddhism; but it is neither *moksha* nor *nirvāna* (see chapter 5).

As this state is often reached by those who have considerable experience in meditation training, it is one that can be objectively studied. There is an extensive literature of over four decades of these studies in India on yogic meditation (e.g., Anand, Chhina, and Singh), in Japan on Zen meditation (e.g., Kasamatsu and Hirai), and by practitioners of Transcendental Meditation in the United States (see summary in Travis and Pearson). Such studies indicate physiological indicators that include changes in EEG, breath rate, skin conductance, and heart rate.

Travis and Pearson (87) suggest that the state is an underlying continuum of the mind "that can be identified in the junction points between waking, dreaming and sleeping," and that the state "can be integrated with waking, dreaming and sleeping." This fits traditions that discuss the state. Chan Buddhism, for example, promotes the state as the ideal continuous state of mind that is achievable with long-term effort but also stresses that there are no stages to this experience; it happens or it does not.

The consciousness-itself state is sometimes confused with the mystic experience, given its contentlessness. In the consciousness-itself state, however, there is no loss of self, as the person is aware of being in the state during the experience and can remember it, even if there is a sense of fundamental non-self. For this reason, one can remain in the state far longer than one can in the mystic experience. Moreover, while those who experience the consciousness-itself state relate feelings of peacefulness and being unbounded, there are not necessarily reports of bliss, of infinite joy, which are common to the mystic experience.

Robert Forman (see also chapter 4), discusses his own pure consciousness experiences arising from Hindu meditation practices. He understands that permanent changes took place in his mental state due to his meditation practices, begun in 1969 and culminating in 1972, that state of mind continuing to at least the date of his writing his book in 1996:

> . . . the feeling inside of being me was like being entirely empty, a perfect vacuum. Since that time all of my thinking, my sensations, my emotions, etc. have seemed not connected to me inside as they once had, for it is as if what was me was now this emptiness. The *silence* was now me, and the thoughts that went on inside have not felt quite in contact with what is really "me," this emptiness. "I" was now silent inside, my thinking has been as if on the outside or somehow in the middle of this silence without quite contacting it. (145)

Given this state of mind, Forman has developed the notion of the "dualistic mystical state" that recognizes that in the state of pure consciousness one is aware of being in the state and can continue to function: "It may be defined as an unchanging interior silence that is maintained concurrently with intentional experience in a long-term or permanent way" (150).

Forman's pure-consciousness state is one that I understand from my own experience and consider to be far from the mystic experience. I began still meditating in 1955 after becoming aware of Buddhism, particularly Chan, on my own, there being no Chan meditation centers in North America at that time. These meditational practices culminated five years later, when I had a number of different types of unitive experiences, never during but after meditation sessions. I then realized that I was more suited to physical modes of meditation and discovered that backpacking in the wilderness with the mind stilled but aware ideally fitted my temperament, but even long walks anywhere would do. This physical mode of meditation reached its culmination in studying *kendo* (Japanese competitive swordsmanship utilizing armor and bamboo approximations of swords) and *iaido* (Japanese swordsmanship using a real sword, of course with no opponent, save for one's self) in Kyoto, alongside Zen monks. I found I was able to successfully function in a no-thought state, essential in order to strike those much more highly trained than oneself. At least from that time, I have remained in a state similar to that described by Forman. Years later, this state of mind was bolstered by an ecstatic realization of the *buddhacitta*, an epiphany that the thinking I experience is not my own but that of the universal Buddha-mind. But to my understanding, this state is neither a unitive experience nor the mystic experience; it is but a ground of existing, of a mental state that has some relationship to such experiences but is not to be confused with the experiences themselves.

THE MYSTIC EXPERIENCE

The mystic experience, as defined in this work, goes beyond unitive experiences and consciousness-itself in that *the experiencer is utterly unaware of the experience at its height.* This is the crucial difference between unitive and mystic experiences. Hence, when understood as union, it is a post facto interpretation of the mystic experience rather than an experience of union in and of itself, save for the fleeting instant prior to the dissolution of self. Thus, the mystic experience differs from all other ecstatic experiences variously included under the rubric of mysticism, because it, and it alone, is utterly ineffable. As there is no experience, from the standpoint of the memory of the experiencer, the crucial part cannot be described whatsoever. The various aspects of the ecstasy that occur just prior to the culmination of the experience are and have been described, as well as the experiences that pertain to returning to consciousness. All else is surmise, save that there is a remarkable similarity (see chapters 5 and 6) in the nature of the conjecture by those who have had the experience to the effect that one actually has experienced the nothingness or total union, involving complete loss of self, that is the ultimate or only reality.

As the mystic experience has been delineated in the preceding chapters, there is no need to repeat the discussion here. The purpose of this chapter is but to contextualize the mystic experience within the types of experiences discussed under the rubric of mysticism in general.

4

Previous Studies

Most studies of mysticism in general, as well as the mystic experience in particular, have been theologically oriented. Accordingly, they have tended to privilege the Western European Christian perspective (see chapter 6) and assume the mystic experience is limited to the "higher religions," meaning the monotheistic ones, with an evolutionary culmination in Christianity. Some studies written from this orientation are still current; for example, Evelyn Underhill's 1910 publication and R. C. Zaehner's 1957 book. The latter was written primarily as a critique of the then understanding of secular, "profane" in Zaehner's rhetoric, mystical experiences. For Zaehner, there are three types of mysticisms, or in terms of this study, mystic experiences: nature, monistic, and theistic. The first he understands to be inferior to both the second and third, and the third, superior to the second. Only "theistic" (meaning monotheistic) mysticism focuses on the love of God, and any other type of mysticism is accordingly inadequate. This position has recently been attacked from the monist point of view by a Hindu analyst, Sutapas Bhattacharya. He posits that theistic religion is incompatible with the perennial wisdom, by which he means the mystic experience. Both are seemingly engaging in childish ethnocentrism: "My mysticism is better than your mysticism."

At the beginning of the twentieth century, studies of mysticism took place in the emerging disciplines, including the humanistic, social scientific, and natural scientific ones. Since the development in the 1960s of religious studies, meaning a comparative and scientific approach to religion in distinction to theology, another disciplinary focus developed, of which this study is an example. These studies attempt to analyze the mystic experience objectively, to varying degrees of success.

The following reflection on previous studies of the mystic experience is meant neither to be comprehensive nor definitive, for this would require a book in itself. Rather the intention is to be suggestive of the directions the various approaches to the study of the mystic experience have taken, as well as to offer critical reflections on these modes of analysis.

PHILOSOPHICAL ANALYSES

If we consider William James's century-old study (see the section on psychological analyses) as a work of psychology rather than philosophy, then the first full-fledged treatment from the perspective of modern philosophy is that of W. T. Stace. As he writes in the preface to his 1960 book, *Mysticism and Philosophy*, "Our predecessors in the field of mysticism have done nothing to help us in many of the problems which I have had to discuss. I have had to chart a lone course without guidance from the past" (7). Unlike his colleagues, he did not dismiss the mystic experience as impossible or unworthy of study. Stace determined that there were two related types of mystical experiences: extrovertive and introvertive. Both share the characteristics of "sense of objectivity or reality," "blessedness, peace, etc.," "feeling of the holy, sacred, or divine," "paradoxicality," and "alleged by mystics to be ineffable." They differ on two criteria: "the Unifying vision—all things are One" and "the more concrete apprehension of the One as an inner subjectivity, or life, in all things" for the extrovertive mystical experience, as compared to "the Unitary Consciousness; the One, the Void; pure consciousness" and "nonspatial, nontemporal" for the introvertive mystical experience" (131). From my own analyses, the first type includes both unitive experiences and the mystic experience where the post facto interpretation has been misunderstood as different from other similar ones. The second type, of course, is the mystic experience.

Stace had been attacked by his colleagues in philosophy even before his seminal work appeared for positions taken in earlier publications, especially with regard to the "alleged ineffability" by those who had the experience. One criticism is that the characteristic is trivial because many types of statements can be analyzed as ineffable from the standpoint of theoretical logic (Gale); another is that the characteristic but labels an experience as impossible (Alston). Most commonly, the continuing criticism has been that thinking takes place solely through language; therefore, there cannot be thoughts that are ineffable. Moreover, an experience that cannot be thought about cannot remain in the memory as experience, nor can an experience logically be nonexperience. The application of any formal logic system to the mystic experience does render the experience theoretically impossible, especially following the development in the mid-twentieth century of strictly focusing philosophical analysis on language.

The problem with this type of formal analysis is that it is irrelevant to the actuality, for people do have the experience. Hence, in the *Zhuangzi* (see Chapters 2 and 5), the emerging school of logic in early China civilization about twenty-four hundred years ago was mocked through satirical depictions of logic-chopping. In the one surviving book from this school of logic (the *Gong Sunlung Zi*), a number of logical statements are demonstrated, the most well-known being: "the set 'white horse' is not equal to the set 'horse'" (*bai ma fei ma*—white horse not horse). The ordinary, literal understanding of the statement is simply the nonsensical, "a white horse is not a horse." The *Zhuangzi* ends one of its satirical discourses with

> To use a finger (characteristic) to demonstrate that fingers (characteristics) are not fingers is not as good as using a nonfinger to demonstrate that fingers are not fingers. To use a horse to demonstrate that a horse is not a horse is not as good as using a non-horse to demonstrate that a horse is not a horse. Sky and Earth are one finger; the myriad things are one horse. (Chapter 2)

This school of logic seems to have lasted but one or two generations. Chinese intellectual culture quickly gave up on formal logic as having any usefulness; it laughed it into oblivion. While it may be logically impossible for me to have had an ineffable experience—ineffable even to myself—for me it remains a fact that I did indeed have it. Thus, I must either give up on myself or formal logic; my own personal choice I trust is obvious.

Stace's volume remained far more popular among those outside of the discipline of philosophy than those within. The understanding that the mystic experience is logically impossible reached its culmination with Steven Katz and those like-minded: ". . . let me state the single epistemological assumption that has exercised my thinking and which has forced me to undertake the present investigation: *There are NO pure (i.e., unmediated) experiences*" (26).

Katz, in arguing that all experiences are culturally mediated, denies that there can be a human experience in and of itself. His argument is particularly directed at Stace, as well as Zaehner, mentioned earlier, and Smart, discussed at the end of this chapter. Stace takes the same position as is presented in the analysis of this work: the mystic experience is essentially the same for all who have it; it is only the postexperience interpretation that may be, and usually is, culturally mediated. Katz's position is not even inherently logical, because his unargued a priori premise necessitates his conclusion. His position does simplify the study of the mystic experience, for he would have us study in detail each traditions' mysticism without any comparison. Hence, from a personal standpoint, Katz not only denies my understanding (and all those with whom I have discussed their own experiences) of the mystic experience, but he denies my scholarly discipline, comparative religion. In stating that, in effect, there is " . . . no foundation for a phenomenology of mysticism or a typology of comparative mystical experience" (56), this book, in effect, is dismissed out of hand.

A somewhat later critique of Stace's position, as influential as Katz's, is that of Wayne Proudfoot, who takes the position that mystical experiences are determined by culture: "These beliefs and attitudes are formative of, rather than consequent upon, the experience. They determine in advance what experiences are possible . . . consequently those in different traditions have different experiences" (121). Proudfoot's thesis collapses when the mystic experience is not understood or interpreted by the experiencer, as is the case for many of the naive examples provided in chapter 2. An experience was had, seemingly identical across cultures, but there is no belief structure to determine the nature of the experience.

The approach of Katz, Proudfoot, and others to mysticism within philosophy of religion has been termed "constructivism": "Constructivism is the view that in significant ways the mystic's conceptual and linguistic scheme determines, shapes, and/or constructs his or her mystical experiences" (Forman 1). Robert Forman, who has had ecstatic experiences, has written a number of critiques of this approach, utilizing the same modes of philosophy as Katz and Proudfoot (he was Proudfoot's student), which is fully realized in his *Mysticism, Mind, Consciousness*.

Perhaps the essential problem with the application of philosophy to an analysis of the mystic experience has been a continuous vague use of the term "mysticism" and a misunderstanding of "mystical experiences." For example, the philosopher of religion Richard Jones, who is quite familiar with the writings of mystics in a number of cultures, uses "mysticism"

> to refer only to the values, action-guides, and belief-commitments constituting those ways of life oriented around experiences (both sensory and introvertive) which lessen the sensory and conceptual structuring of ordinary experiences and thereby allegedly permit an insight into the nature of reality. (59)

Jones conceives "mystical experiences" to "result from a process. . . . " (1). Thus, mysticism is not understood as the experiences in and of themselves, and the experiences are understood as being due to conscious effort. Such a terminological basis is not going to lead to analyses relevant to the mystic experience per se.

PSYCHOLOGICAL ANALYSES

In my last quarter as an undergraduate psychology major at the University of Chicago in the spring of 1960, I took a directed reading course on "Psychology and Mysticism." After finding an apathetic faculty member to theoretically guide me, there being no one in the psychology department interested in the subject matter, I devoured everything written on the topic in English to that date. Other than some psychotherapists whose knowledge of the topic was solely based on reading D. T. Suzuki's writings on Zen Buddhism, popular among intellectuals in the 1950s, the only psychologist to write on the topic positively, who did not consider mysticism within the rubric of psychopathology, was among the first to do so and first psychologists, William James. This course resulted in my terminating the formal study of psychology, and I subsequently shifted my academic affiliation to religious studies and East Asia.

A century has passed since William James's 1902 pioneering work, along with Starbuck's 1899 study, and, shockingly, it remains the best psychological study to date. (Since James was a philosopher as well as a psychologist, psychology developing out of philosophy, and published books on both psychology and philosophy, some scholars consider his work on religious experience to be within the philosophy of religion rather than psychology; I believe James would disagree, given he has a separate section on philosophy in the work.) The work is still in print and continues to be the subject of approving study (e.g., Barnard).

Among the types of experiences discussed in James's *The Varieties of Religious Experience*, there is a section on "Mysticism." He enumerates four characteristics of such experiences: 1) Ineffability; 2) Noetic quality, "they carry with them a curious sense of authority for after-time"; 3) Transiency, lasting for but a half hour to an hour or so; and 4) Passivity, as if the experiencer's "own will were in abeyance." The problem with his analyses, one common to many studies, is that all the varieties of ecstatic experience are confused. James does write about various types of mystic experience, but the categories can place together, for example, shamanistic phenomena with the mystic experience itself. Where James does write with a clearer assurance is when he discusses experiences induced by nitrous oxide (laughing gas), a substance commonly used by dentists at the time as an anesthetic, in which he himself had indulged.

In a half-century later, more comprehensive psychological study, Arbman's massive three-volume *Ecstasy or Religious Trance*, the same problem mitigates the value of the work in regard to our topic: various types of ecstatic experience are confused together. Thus, the question may arise, is it important, from the psychological perspective, to delineate the various types of ecstatic experiences as is carried out in chapter 3 of this work? From my own personal experiences in all the modes discussed in that chapter save for spirit possession, and from conversations with shamans and mediums who also had the mystic and other ecstatic experiences (see chapter 5), I have no doubt that these involve different mental states, and, to a degree, involve different aspects of the brain, and so forth. Accordingly, a psychology which does not deal with these differences is too imprecise to inform our understanding with regard to the specific ecstatic state of the mystic experience.

With regard to the mystic experience itself, Arbman has confused it with Christian unitive experiences, thus arguing that to understand that "the mystic's ego-consciousness has been dissolved, absorbed and entirely lost . . ." is incorrect (II: 382). Such rhetoric is rare among Christian mystics for theological reasons, but it does exist (see chapter 6). It is not a case, as Arbman assumes, that there is a kind of dual consciousness in which the experiencer is conscious of loss of ego in union (and mystic) experiences; Forman (see earlier and chapter 3) also makes such an argument, but for a continuing nonecstatic sense of non-self. Those who have the mystic experience, rather, are only aware of loss of self—or absorption into the Godhead for Roman Catholics—on coming out of the experience and reflecting on the memory of what precedes the "nothingness" experience; they are not conscious of loss of self after the self is lost.

Until the 1960s, the psychological study of the mystic experience was considerably influenced by psychoanalysis. It is often assumed that Sigmund Freud termed the experience as "oceanic," but he was referring, in his *Civilization and Its Discontents*, to a feeling "as of something limitless, unbounded, something 'oceanic'" that is continuous, not a temporary ecstatic state: "So it is a feeling of indissoluble connection, of belonging inseparably to the external world, as a whole" (8–9). Nonetheless, it seems likely that Freud would also have applied the same understanding to the mystic experience. For he considered it infantile regression, a return to or continuation of a state of the utterly immature human being; in effect, a return to the id. Freud was very much a product of Enlightenment thinking and unlikely to value a state of consciousness that he would understand as ultimately irrational.

Carl Jung has written a number of prefaces and analyses of "Eastern" religious writings assumed to be mystical. But he did so after developing his theories of the collective unconscious and of archetypes, and after working out his psychotherapeutic goal of individuation. Thus, he interpreted this literature from the standpoint of his theoretical framework, rather than allow this literature to inform and possibly shape his understanding; hence, the literature was perceived as but reinforcing his own theories (see expanded critique in Jones 169–83).

One of the founders of humanistic, or "third force" (the first two being Freudian and experimental-behavioristic) psychology, Abraham Maslow published in 1964 a slim volume based on a lecture entitled *Religions, Values, and Peak-Experiences*, that continues in current interest. Rather than basing his theories on psychopathologies, as did virtually all other theorists of personality at the time, he focused on exceptionally healthy individuals, those who led happy, fulfilling lives. What he found is that such persons had been influenced by what he called "peak-experiences," which led to "self-actualization." Peak-experiences would include the mystic experience but also unitive and other similar experiences that may or may not occur in a nominally religious milieu. These experiences are central to the development of a healthy, fully actualized personality. In a preface to the volume added a half-dozen years later, Maslow cautioned that such experiences could lead a person to continue to seek and exclusively focus on them to the detriment of a more holistic approach to understanding and life.

This positive approach to ecstatic religious experiences led to developments in psychology that came to be termed "transpersonal psychology" in 1975. One of the founders of this movement, Charles Tart, had earlier published an influential anthology, *Altered States of Consciousness*, with a large number of articles and excerpts approaching trance states from many social scientific perspectives. Transpersonal psychology focuses on spiritual development, brings various spiritual practices into psychotherapy, and in seeking to understand spiritual experiences scientifically, has a tendency to accept varying statements from non-Western religious traditions undiscriminatingly, while taking a highly critical attitude toward Western religions.

Currently, one of the most influential transpersonal psychologists, Ken Wilber, assumes a unitary perennial wisdom flowing from the assumed same religious experiences to be at the base of all religions, as did Maslow. But Wilber understands these experiences necessarily to occur in a hierarchical series, peaking in a Hindu monistic experience, rather than ecstatic experiences occurring randomly and variously among individuals.

Another influential transpersonal psychologist, Stanislav Grof (*Psychology* 289), adds a generalized theistic twist to the mystic experience that the word "transcendental" can imply:

> They become aware of the fact that the undifferentiated Absolute Consciousness/Void represents not only the end of the spiritual journey, but also the source and beginning of creation. The Divine is the principle offering reunion for the separated, but also the agent responsible for the division and separation of the original unity. If this principle were complete and self-fulfilling in its pristine form, there would be not be any reason for it to create and the other experiential realms would not exist.

It is the assumption of will and need with regard to the ultimate that anthropomorphizes the concept.

The fundamental difficulties in transpersonal psychology's incorporation of spirituality into psychotherapy with regard to understanding the mystic experience is the attempt to homogenize all ecstatic religious experiences and the cultural interpretations of them into a single understanding and to take the various understandings, at times misunderstood due to poor translations, as an unfiltered source for the creation of scientific paradigms. Concerning the relating of ecstatic religious experiences to psychotherapy, particularly the mystic experience, the nonpredictability of the experience renders such techniques rather dubious. The very concept of "transpersonal" in transpersonal psychology negates an analysis of the experience as one of an event in the brain, and so it is to the emerging neurosciences (see the section on biological analyses) that we must turn for such an analysis.

The modern West is not the only culture in which psychology developed. Due to their interest in meditation for a specific purpose, Buddhists early developed psychological analyses of ecstatic experiences, particularly of stages that take place during particular experiences. In the Buddhist psychological paradigm, "the eight stages of trance," the eighth stage is "passing beyond the field of nothing whatever, he dwells in the attainment of the station of neither perception nor non-perception" (Conze, *Buddhist Meditation* 118).

This is a statement regarding a mental state that is relatively concise, clear, and to the point. It is a state that, being the culmination of mental and spiritual development, is understood to be rare and not linked to therapy.

SOCIOLOGICAL ANALYSES

There have been a number of sociological surveys, especially in North America, of attitudes toward religion, variously defined but usually from a relatively fundamentalist Christian perspective, including religious experience. The surveys that include the latter tend to indicate that the majority of those surveyed understand themselves to have had such experiences. But without in-depth interviews based on questions drawn up by sociologists who understand ecstatic religious experiences, the results are too amorphous to allow for any certainty in these regards.

There are exceptions to the above critique, especially the ground-breaking survey, sampling nearly fifteen hundred respondents, carried out by the National Opinion Research Center and analyzed by the eminent sociologist of religion, Andrew Greeley. The study covered not only religious experiences, but psychic experiences and experiences with the dead. Two general conclusions arose from the study:

1. The paranormal is normal. Psychic and mystic experiences are frequent even in modern urban industrial society. The majority of the population has had some such experience, a substantial minority has had more than just an occasional experience, and a respectable proportion of the population has such experiences frequently . . .
2. People who have paranormal experiences, even frequent [sic] such experiences, are not kooks. They are not sick, they are not deviants, they are not social misfits, they are not schizophrenics, they are not drug freaks. In fact they may be more emotionally healthy than those who do not have such experiences. (7)

There was a general question (followed up by in-depth interviews) regarding "mystical" experiences, which was well worded to ascertain ecstatic experiences while avoiding religious bias: "Have you ever felt as though you were very close to a powerful, spiritual force that seemed to lift you out of yourself?" (58). Thirty-six percent of the sample responded positively to the question, with over 30 percent in every age group. When correlated with religious affiliation, 43 percent of Protestants responding answered positively,

29 percent of Jews, and but 24 percent of Catholics, as compared to 45 percent for "other" and 29 percent for "none."

Greeley realized that "The most serious weakness in the whole research enterprise reported here is that our question designed to determine whether a respondent had an 'ecstatic' experience may not in fact measure real ecstasy but only heightened emotion" (77). Applying factor analysis to particular descriptor items relating to William James's and others' characteristics of mysticism, including experiencing "being bathed in light," it was determined that 52 percent of those responding positively to the general question met at least some of the characteristics, and 40 percent had all four. This means that 19 percent of all those surveyed had an experience that would correlate with one of the experiences discussed in the second half of chapter 3, and 14 percent had an experience at least close to the mystic experience.

The biologist Alister Hardy, in establishing the Religious Experience Research Centre, created a pool of data from which sociological analyses have been drawn, including his own study, *The Spiritual Nature of Man*. This database is more useful than most surveys as there are no questions presented that in themselves potentially bias or skew the data, although this criticism is not directed toward the National Opinion Research Center survey discussed earlier. It is the Religious Experience Research Centre's database that partially informs chapters 2 and 3 of this study.

ANTHROPOLOGICAL ANALYSES

While there are a plethora of anthropological studies of functional ecstasy, the only anthropologist to focus on the mystic experience in and of itself has been Agehananda Bharati, whose experience and theories were briefly mentioned in chapter 2. Bharati had a most unusual career. An Austrian, in his youth during World War II he learned to speak several Indian languages, and after the war he went to India, where he studied Hindu tantrism and became one of the few non-Indians to not only be accepted as a Hindu in India, but a guru as well (see his autobiography, *The Ochre Robe*). He then went to the United States, where he studied anthropology at the University of Washington and then joined the anthropology faculty at Syracuse University. He was one of the founding members of the Society for the Scientific Study of Religion.

In his *The Light at the Center*, Bharati anchors his analysis of the mystic experience on his own experiences, one of which he had at the age of twelve and a second after he mastered tantric practices, that is, in relationship to sexual experience. Thus his understanding is not based on surmise, as are most published studies of the mystic experience, or on hiding a personal understanding. Unfortunately, the work is highly flawed, and his understanding of the topic never received the hearing which it was due. Part of the problem with the study is that two different but related topics were uncomfortably merged together: an anthropological study of the mystic experience, which Bharati terms the "zero-experience," and a critique of modern Hinduism from one who is part of the phenomenon. Second, the work seems to have been dictated without tight editing, and it is highly repetitious. Finally, the anthropological analysis is imbued with a Hindu understanding of the phenomenon when the author is attempting to deal with the zero-experience from a nonculturally specific perspective. For example, Bharati has little understanding of functional ecstasies and confuses spirit possession trance with the mystic experience. Nonetheless, it remains to date the only comprehensive study based on actual experiences by a social scientist who understands the experience. I have personally benefited from this study and occasional conversations I had with him throughout the 1970s.

Among the points Bharati makes about the mystic experience, several differ from the received wisdom in this regard, but they are points that clear up serious misconceptions and resonate with my own experiences and those of others with whom I have discussed them. One point is that having had the experience, "I do not hanker after the experience—it is non-addictive to me" (46). This does not mean that one would not enjoy having it again, but that there is not a driving need to repeat the experience. I go further than Bharati in suggesting that the "dark night of the soul" is not the norm. Most traditions expect the person who has had the experience to return to the world and continue to function rather than spend the rest of one's life seeking to repeat it. Another point is that "the zero-experience comes to those to whom it comes, regardless of what they do; it also comes, I believe, to those few who try very hard over a long period of time" (65).

The first part of this point is also made in the *Zhuangzi* and in several other traditions. I myself am uncertain as to the second part, but given Bharati is part of a tradition that understands that intense training over decades can lead to it, its inclusion is understandable.

The most controversial point is that the mystic experience does not lead to sainthood, that a despicable person can have the experience and remain despicable afterward:

I can only say that we know these two facts: 1) that the zero-
experience invades the person's ego-perspective, changing him in
few ways not predictable from his previous career, though his style
of reporting may be predictable from antecedents in his culture;
2) that it does nothing to the person in his interactional patterns
with other people and with human society at large. (100)

Speaking for myself, I do not think the experience changed me in the
slightest in the latter regard, although it thoroughly reinforced my Buddho-
Daoist understanding of the nature of reality. Anyone who knows me can
assuredly verify that I am hardly a saint.

COMBINED APPROACHES:
ANTHROPOLOGY AND PSYCHOLOGY

The best analyses of ecstatic states in general tend to be by scholars who utilize multiple methodologies. None of these studies, save the present one, have
approached the topic of the mystic experience as all such studies focus on
functional ecstasies. Three will be briefly mentioned as examples.

Wolfgang Jilek, an ethnopsychiatrist, was trained as both a psychiatrist
and an anthropologist. He spent many years working with the inland Salish in
British Columbia and presents a sympathetic study of their healing ceremonies
in *Salish Indian Mental Health and Culture Change* (an expanded study was reti-
tled *Indian Healing*). In the third chapter, Jilek concisely presents the best psy-
chobiological analysis of the triggers to shamanistic trance to date. Daniel
Merkur's, *Becoming Half Hidden: Shamanism and Initiation Among the Inuit*, written from a history of religions perspective, combines a thorough study of the
ethnographic record by ethnologists with psychological analysis to come up
with a most insightful understanding of shamanistic training and initiation, at
least for the Inuit. Michael Winkelman, an anthropologist, in an article on
trance states, provides psychophysiological models of functional ecstatic states
that brings the neurosciences, discussed later, into ethnological studies.

BIOLOGICAL ANALYSES

Given that the mystic experience is a mental experience and, therefore, one
that takes place in the brain, then, from the modern biological understanding

of the brain, the experience must minimally be understood as an electro-chemical event in the brain. Hence, one would expect that the developing neurophysiological theories should be most fruitful in expanding our understanding of the nature of the experience. I use the word "theories" as direct research on the mystic experience would be impossible given its infrequency in any particular individual.

Unfortunately, until the late 1990s, the major and best known publications on the topic promised much but were woefully lacking. There was a tendency for practicing psychiatrists to write on the subject whose understanding of religion was limited to early twentieth-century studies (e.g., the long since discredited "myth and religion" school) and whose knowledge of neuroscientific research was shockingly abysmal. Many of the studies were written by seemingly fundamentalist Christian physicians literally looking for "God in the brain." This God was the Christian one in all of its doctrinal ramifications. Some thought they had found the precise location where the explicit message of Jesus Christ as Son of God was hardwired into the brain. This meant, of course, that only conservative Christians were fully human beings; and there were no physiologically complete human beings prior to the inception of Christian creeds. Even the Medieval Inquisition did not go that far; they perversely followed normative Christian theology, which holds that humans have free will and have to chose through faith the Christian truth. Arnold Mandell, in a 1980 publication, dealt with the theme, "God in the Brain," in the title of his article, but he was looking for a neurological explanation of transcendence in general. And that was his problem, for transcendence is far too broad a category to find a single explanation. Mandell comes up with a hodge-podge of possibilities with little coherence. (For a further critique, see Austin 184.)

The late Eugene d'Aquili, with various coauthors, had been writing on religion and psychobiology for a couple of decades (see 1979). In his 1990 book, void consciousness is specifically discussed, but it is understood not as an experience but a state of cognitive development: ". . . sufficiently matured in their development that this advanced knowing may arise." This state is understood as "a permanent stage in the development of the perceiver's neurocognitive system" (Laughlin Jr. 333).

In his last work, published posthumously in 1999 with Andrew Newberg, d'Aquili is forthcoming about a bias in his works I suspected when I first came upon them nearly a quarter-century ago. While the title, *The Mystical Mind: Probing the Biology of Religious Experience*, explicitly places the work in the context of biology, the introduction clearly states that the book is a theological treatise, not one within religious or neurophysiological studies: "We intend to present here the most comprehensive metatheology to date" (7). Typical of their gross ignorance of religion, the authors assume that Hinduism and implicitly Buddhism are monotheistic, that dervishes "rapidly" whirl themselves into a trance (obviously, d'Aquili had never observed a Sufi ritual), and they describe "voodoo frenzy" (are Hollywood fantasies a valid source of religious data?). Given that the authors taught or teach psychiatry at the University of Pennsylvania Medical School, we should at least expect the neuroscience aspect to be useful. While a history of this field is surveyed, the authors' focus on creating diagrams of the mind based on vague models of the workings of the brain reminiscent of the transpersonal psychologist Charles Tart's (*States of Consciousness*) diagrams of several decades ago that have little if any actual connection to neuroscientific research.

D'Aquili and Newberg posit that there are two systems in the brain: arousal and quiescent systems. When both are maximally discharged, the net result is the *unio mystica* or void consciousness. The authors discuss how the mind creates myth, which necessarily points to a monotheistic god—for the authors, there are only five religions in the entire world: Christianity, Judaism, Islam, Hinduism, and Buddhism, all, in effect, interpreted as a modes of Christianity: ". . . the concepts of a Christ figure or a solar hero represent cognitive solutions within the myth [in general] to the problem by the basically antinomous myth structure" (87). Hence, Christ, in effect, is programmed in the brain itself. Myth, according to the authors, is only meaningful when it is enacted in ritual: "It is because of the reciprocal representation of the content of the major neural systems that human beings are naturally disposed to act out their myths" (88). By ritual, the authors primarily mean meditation. Even in this regard, rather than rely on actual meditation practices in various religions, the evidence presented are experiments from several decades ago, such as those of Deikman. The "ultimate trance state" arising from meditation is the experience of the "Ultimate Absolute Being," that is, God. Anything else is a "lesser mystical state." Complex charts of the workings of the brain are presented to somehow scientifically prove God in the brain.

Given the authors evolutionary framework, it is hardly surprising that they find that when the brain functions totally we have "the high Western religions—Judaism, Islam, and Christianity." But all religions are ultimately Christian: "Mystics of all religions achieve an immediate sense of God via the total application of the holistic operator to the totality of reality." The last sentence serves as an exemplar of their neuropsychology, about which no more need be said. This leads to their positing the only valid theology, which they call "neurotheology": "We feel certain, however, that any specific theological idea may eventually be reducible to neurophysiological functions" (175). They conclude with a presentation of their "megatheology": ". . . a megatheology should contain content of such a universal nature that it could be adopted by most, if not all, of the world's great religions as a basic element without any serious violation of their essential doctrines" (198). And what is this megatheology? Why the monotheistic, Christian God in the brain, of course. (For a further critique, focusing on d'Aquili's use of the neurosciences, see Watts 334–37.)

Other analysts have not been as Eurocentric in linking theology to the neurosciences, even in works sponsored by the Vatican. For example, Wesley Wildman, a theologian, teamed up with Leslie Brothers, a research psychiatrist, to summarize the possible relationships to date between the neurosciences, studies in semiotics, and religious experience. Their ultimate conclusion is theological, but from as broad a perspective as theologically possible:

> . . . there is something out there and in here. . . . This ultimate *something* that we sense in the depths of nature is not much like a personal God. . . . It is not even much like a being. Yet it is not nothing either, even if Buddhists are right to say that it is somehow indeterminate or empty. It *is* real, and it is doubtless more than wondrous and strange than our best and worst guesses. This is the hypothesis that makes sense of the best data, including the data on religious experience. (413)

Fortunately, a massive tome (well over eight hundred pages) has relatively recently appeared by an author, James Austin, who is highly qualified, with many decades of experience in both neuroscientific research and Zen Buddhist meditational practice, and has had a number of different kinds of ecstatic religious experiences himself. In his work, he lays out in detail the state of the neurosciences and the practices of Zen—it is an excellent introduction to both—before combining the two together.

Following Zen theory, Austin terms the mystic experience "Ultimate Being, beyond expression," which involves an awareness of "primordial emptiness, a groundless void beyond oneness" as the most highly intense experience (303). It is posited as the eighth state of nine in meditational progress, the last three states being "advanced extraordinary alternate states of consciousness":

The next rare state is VIII, Ultimate Being. Capital letters are often used in association with the phrase. They do little more than hint at its inexpressible properties. This state of grace is reserved for the very few. They are persons who are far advanced in their practice of the spiritual path, and who have previously undergone several awakenings. (304)

The author here is reflecting the Buddhist perspective (see chapter 5), but as has been argued in this study, the experience is infrequent but not rare, and it is not directly related to meditational practices. Nor would I claim it to be "advanced."

Austin analyzes the various constituents of the experience (as delineated in chapter 1) from the standpoint of the neurosciences. Regarding the experience of light, he notes that in his own experience, during a shift from light to deep sleep,

> the lateral geniculate cells discharge, stimulated by acetylcholine [ACH] cells down in the brain stem. So a plausible explanation for the light is a sudden surge in firing. First, it causes an excessive degree of visual transmission. Then, as it spreads farther, it generates a sense of "envelopment." (376)

For the general experience of the light, Austin notes that, "The basic fact, of course, is that many more visual impulses relay through the lateral geniculate nucleus *when the brain is in transition to its desynchronized states.*" This would fit my own experience described in chapter 1: "Moreover, these brief moments of drowsiness are especially prone to enhance visual transmission if, at the same time, the midbrain reticular formation is then stimulated" (377). The author then proceeds to detail the ACH pathways and receptors.

Emptiness is understood, using the terms of this study, as self-loss, or as Austin expresses it, "the absence of the psychic self" (570). He nuances various aspects of emptiness, some of which are more germane to the consciousness-itself state discussed in the previous chapter than the mystic experience. Austin's discussion of the third aspect of emptiness is more relevant to the latter:

> It is nothing less than a state of groundlessness which lies altogether beyond. . . . It stretches our everyday intellectual processes too far to ask them to grasp a state which is, simultaneously, both an emptiness *and* the absolute reality of all things. (571)

The mystic experience and other related experiences as the consciousness-itself state are understood by Austin to involve the following neurological mechanisms:

1. A brisk conjunction of certain acetylcholine and glutamate activating functions.
2. Interactions cosponsored among major thalmic nuclei and their cortical counterparts, both in the frontotemporal and parieto-occipital regions.
3. A dropping out of many of the usual temporal lobe, limbic, central grey, and medial orbito-frontal functions.
4. A possible enhancement of certain peptide-related functions within these and other specified regions. (614)

Added to this is the possibility that "mu receptors, responding to a covert earlier event, and acted upon by beta-endorphin and enkephalins, are candidated for contributing climates of additional depth and scope to the resonances of immanence, ultimate perfection, and eternity" (620).

As a final fillip, Austin suggests that spring and its release from seasonal depression, as well as increased sunshine and warmth may play a role:

We now know that when hibernating animals stir from their ice-like state, the nerve cells at the leading edge of this springtime awakening are those in the hippocampus and hypothalamus. Further research into human biorhythms and cyclic events may help define more precisely why some mornings, and the late spring months, could tend to be more open to states of spiritual renewal. (621)

My own mystic experience took place in the late spring while lying in the warm sun during mid-day in a state of hyper-relaxation.

Another aspect of biology, aside from the neurosciences, are sex-gender considerations. In an earlier publication (*Through the Earth*), based on extensive ethnographic material, as well as discussions with female mediums and shamans, the point is made that females are more easily able to enter into mediumistic and shamanistic ecstatic states than males. Furthermore, I suggested that this difference is due to differences in brain structure, and some genetic markers are starting to be identified in this regard. Lene Sjørup, who also investigated the Religious Experience Research Centre's archives, noted that the vast majority of self-reports were from women. After reading her article, I realized that virtually all of those students who reported having the mystic experience to me over many years were also female. It seems that females are not just more prone to functional ecstatic states than males but to ecstatic states in general. Neurological research that took sexual differentiation into account undoubtedly could further elucidate the biological nature of the experience.

NEAR-DEATH EXPERIENCE STUDIES

Related to biological studies are studies of phenomena similar to those of certain ecstatic religious experiences that have occurred to some people who have been close to death, or whose hearts were not beating for a short time but were not brain-dead, termed the "near-death experience" (NDE) in the literature. Although the subject had been written about for many years prior to Raymond Moody's *Life after Life*, it was this slim volume, and a number of others by the same author that followed, which focused attention on NDEs. *Life after Life* has been in print for a quarter of a century and has sold several million copies. Over the last quarter century, there have been a number of studies, both popular and scientific, on the topic, and there are national and international associations for near-death studies. These developments through the mid-80s have been analyzed by Carol Zaleski, who also compares the modern material with medieval descriptions of otherworld journeys.

The focus of most of these studies has been the verification of life after death for the more general interpretations, and the proven reality of the popular notion of the Christian life after death for the more theological ones. For example, a relatively recent work by two established sociologists concludes:

> Near-death research has shed new understanding on this early life and its meaning and purpose as well as on the previous life and the life to come. In essence, this body of scientific data provides what appears to be newly discovered, or possibly rediscovered, truth that suggests life did not begin at mortal birth, nor does it end at mortal death, also that human development and progress did not begin at birth and will not end at death. (Lundhal and Widdison 266)

This is a very reassuring message indeed for the majority of modern Westerners who no longer primarily rely on theological understandings but on popularized scientific ones. It is also a message that has been reiterated by Hollywood films based, in part, on the popularization of NDE studies.

Estimates of the number of persons near death who have such experiences range between 35 percent (Gallup) and 22 percent (Roberts and Owen); the latter focused on whether or not the person was actually very near death based on medical considerations. Given the medical context of these experiences and their similarity to experiences while not under physical duress, it is possible that understanding the physiological circumstances can further our understanding of the biological aspects of ecstatic religious experiences.

According to the Gallup survey based on personal interviews with fifteen hundred adults, the most common experiences involve varying types of out-of-body experiences; that is, seeing one's body from a viewpoint away from one's body, usually above, and/or feeling separated from one's body. These experiences most closely relate to shamanistic phenomena. More germane to the mystic experience are the experiences of being enveloped in a bright, colorless light and traveling, often in a tunnel, faster and faster away from one's body, a journey that the person realizes they can and do stop—at least for those who did not actually die. Alternately, persons may experience the beginning of the dissolution of identity, often combined with the feeling of merging with infinity (God for those theologically inclined), again with the choice made to not totally lose oneself but to return to life. More recent studies indicate that those who have the "light" experience are those who were closest to death from the medical perspective (Owens, Cook, and Stevenson).

The sole neurological analysis of this phenomena in relation to the mystic experience is by Austin (444), who finds, from the medical perspective, that the persons having NDEs had "some disorder of their cerebral functioning. That is, they were drowning, oxygen-deprived, in vasomotor shock with low blood pressure, or otherwise seriously ill." Austin (451) tentatively suggests a neurological scenario for NDEs, which correlate to his analysis (see earlier in this chapter) of the mystic and related experiences without trauma:

> A synaptic turmoil occurs during the first seconds of a major near-death experience. It will quickly release, *into the brain*, biogenic armines and peptides. Impulses racing through the deeper visual pathways could generate a sense of light. And other events will be set in motion which extend their influences as low as the medulla. Here, for example, lie such large cells as those of the

paragigantocellular nucleus . . . if the injured person's blood pressure were to drop, some large cells in this nucleus would also fire, as part of the usual reflex response set up to raise low blood pressure back up toward normal levels. Within milliseconds, impulses rising from this paragigantocellular nucleus would travel the short distance up to the locus ceruleus. Here, they would prompt its cells to release their norepinephrine throughout the central nervous system. This NE would help set off another major round of the brain's own stress responses . . . [that] influence functions at many levels, including those powerful functions of the hypothalamus.

COMPARATIVE RELIGION STUDIES

A scholar of Indian philosophy rather than a comparative religionist, Fritz Staal wrote *Exploring Mysticism*, a study of the study of mysticism without a Western bias. It is a good introduction to the study of mysticism to its date of writing a quarter century ago, although its focus, of course, is on the South Asian understanding. Being familiar with nontheistic traditions, Staal clearly understands that ecstatic experiences are a function of the mind. The one aspect of his study with which I would disagree is the need for "contemplation under the guidance of a guru," at least for the mystic experience. The need for a guru is indicative of the influence of Hinduism and is not found in other cultures.

Staal's study also reflects the then current interest in the relationship between mysticism and the use of psychoactive substances, which is of limited relevance to the mystic experience per se. I have yet to meet anyone who has had the mystic experience triggered by the ingestion of a psychoactive substance, although the use of such substances can lead to unitive experiences.

Also a specialist in Hinduism, Ninian Smart is one of the founders of religious studies, and his approach to our topic is invariably comparative. In an early study (1965), Smart treats mysticism "as primarily consisting of an interior or introvertive quest, culminating in certain interior experiences which are not described in terms of sense-experiences or of mental images, etc." (75). This article is primarily an attack on Zaehner, mentioned at the beginning of this chapter, but his conclusions have wider ramifications. Smart understands that "phenomenologically, mysticism is everywhere the same," and that "different flavors accrue to the experiences of mystics because of the ways of life and modes of auto-interpretation" (87).

An interesting and quite different comparative approach to the topic is Jeffrey Kripal's recent *Roads of Excess, Palaces of Wisdom: Eroticism and Reflexivity in the Study of Mysticism*. Kripal studies those who have studied mysticism and also seem to have had ecstatic experiences, including Underhill, Zaehner, and Bharati discussed earlier, as well as Wolfson, whose work is utilized in chapter 6. Kripal stresses a point opposite to my own viewpoint, as he argues that those who study mysticism tend to do so because of their own personal experiences. For those on whom Kripal focuses his attention, not excluding himself, his point is well taken. That is, regarding those who accept the reality of the mystic experience, I am in full accord with Kripal. It is with regard to those who deny the existence of the experience that I assume there has been no such experience.

The present work is another example of a comparative religion approach to the topic. It is in full accord with Smart's general conclusion above.

5

Ethnohermeneutics I: Non-West

SHAMANISTIC AND MEDIUMISTIC TRADITIONS

Little is available on the incidence of the mystic experience in most of the religions of the world—including the indigenous religions of sub-Saharan Africa, Native America (North and South), Australia, and far northern Eurasia—for a number of reasons. First, many of these traditions were, until modern times, nonliterate, and actual oral spiritual traditions are difficult to access. Second, these traditions focus on religion with regard to pragmatic needs, such as subsistence, healing, and protection; religious experience accordingly centers on functional ecstasies, such as shamanistic and mediumistic ones.

As we shall see, only when a tradition has sufficient agricultural surplus to allow for a nonproducing class—whether of warriors, priests, or a combination of the two—do we find a cultural interest in nonfunctional ecstatic experiences. That is, there has to be a group of persons, usually hereditary, who are not expected by the culture to engage in farming, and other forms of labor, so as to allow for periods of total leisure when the bliss of the mystic experience may be deliberately sought or celebrated. The Mesoamerican and Andean civilizations would have fit such a category but the libraries of the former were destroyed soon after their conquest by Europeans, and the latter did not have writing. In any case, the aristocratic religious modes disappeared under colonialism, and only the pragmatic aspects of the religion among the nonaristocracy has continued to the present.

As chapter 2 demonstrated, the mystic experience occurs among at least a few of all peoples and cultures and probably considerably more. The question to be considered now is not whether they occur but how they are understood. Where we do have ethnographic and other sources for examples of the mystic experience in shamanistic traditions, they are separate from or adjunct to the functional trances of shamanism.

Knut Rasmussen traveled among the Inuit and interviewed their shamans in the early twentieth century, long before they were forced by the American, Canadian, Danish, and Russian governments to reside in fixed settlements having a strong Christian missionary presence, with major changes in their lifestyle and religion. In his writings, there is an example of a person who perhaps had the mystic experience, or at least aspects of it, and understood the experience as a source of shamanistic power, but not a shamanistic trance in and of itself:

> Every real shaman has to feel an illumination in his body, in the inside of his head or in his brain, something that gleams like fire, that gives him the power to see with closed eyes into the darkness, into the hidden things or into the future, or into the secrets of another man. I felt that I was in possession of this marvelous ability. (240–41 in Lommel 60)

This was the ecstatic experience that began this individual's career as a shaman; he then goes on to detail his accumulation of the necessary tutelary spirits for shamanistic functioning. The Inuit's experience suggests that the mystical experience does indeed take place in shamanistic culture but is not in itself a shamanistic experience, it having no social function, one of the deterministic criteria according to Hultkrantz and the factor by which Helmut Hoffman (103), discussing Tibetan religion, distinguishes the mystic from the shaman:

> The shaman establishes his connection with the supernatural world in trance not for the sake of his personal experience (like the mystic or ecstatic of almost all higher religions) but for the well-being of his group. (Translated from German)

A former undergraduate and graduate student of mine, whose mother is Ojibwe, had been "trained" by the shaman John-Paul, who, until the revitalization beginning in the late 1970s, was considered the last in the Manitoulin area (north shore of Lake Superior). Marilyn Johnson's training began during the year preceding his death in 1976.

In an introduction to an undergraduate paper (quoted with permission) written decades ago, she presented a typology of ascent experiences as imparted to her by John-Paul:

"Flights" serve three purposes:

1. To inspect the physical and emotional well-being of friends, relatives, and other individuals under one's care. A shaman can be a spiritual guardian for people he has met or people he has never physically met but who are of specific interest to him; e.g., future trainees for shamanism. If the shaman cannot physically be in a specific place, then he can still check on a particular individual who may be far away.
2. To seek the advice from the spirit (soul) of one's ancestors or from the spirits of other departed individuals, or to obtain information from them about a particular person or event in one's life.
3. A "flight" to the place where the spirit abides ("Paradise"). One seeks a harmonizing union of pure spirit, the purpose being one of revitalization of spirit and body; i.e., a revitalization of power.

In the third type of flight, the spirit travels westward [traditional direction of the abode of the dead] to "Paradise." The spirit upon arrival meets the Spirit which appears in the form of a brilliant ball of light—sometimes glowing white or with golden hues. Then a harmonizing union of the Spirit and the spiritual essence of the shaman takes place.

The shaman experiences a fulfilled nothingness state; he is not aware of anything—there exists a fulfilled void or holistic emptiness. Then one catches a glimpse of the "earth" below and the spirit must return to physical reality. The descent then takes place and the return is immediate. The shaman comes out of the trance feeling peaceful, full of power, and numb for a short period as the body awakens; there is a great feeling of revitalization.

John-Paul of the Birch Island Reserve (just north of Manitoulin Island) was born in the early part of the twentieth century, the son and grandson of shamans, the latter being the famous nineteenth-century shaman, Shaw-wan-oss-way. I have been given two estimates of John-Paul's age at death in 1976: mid-sixties and mid-seventies. His father and grandfather had undergone the vision-quest, but he had not. (Data for the life of John-Paul is from personal communication in 1978 with Professor J. E. Newberry of the University of Sudbury and Leona Nawagebow of the Birch Island Reserve.)

In the early part of the twentieth century, vision-questing was dying out among the Anishnabe. Landes (*Prairie* 183) reports that among the Potawatomi in the mid-1930s, an informant told her that the "obligation had waned before 1920, though the practice had lingered." Rogers (*Round Lake* D5) reports that in the late '50's among the Western Ontario Ojibwe, "informants stated most emphatically that this is no longer practiced and they themselves have never been on an *antapawamo* [vision-quest]."

Even the influence of dreaming had been waning due to the changed ecological circumstances—"I did not follow up my dreams because I lived like a white man" (Landes, *Prairie* 195)— although it had far from disappeared. Radin ("Ojibwa" 233) provides examples, from the beginning of the nineteenth to the early twentieth centuries, demonstrating that, "as the puberty fasting experience lost its social significance, dreams, in general, lost theirs. . . ."

Instead, John-Paul's "calling" came slightly later in life when, in his twenties, on a boat in the midst of a thunderstorm, a vision was induced by a lightning flash—Ojibwe shamans often derive their power from the thunder spirit. He then began to function as a shaman. Hence, he gained his status by all three means of early twentieth-century Ojibwe culture, "by means of dreams, by inheritance through the male line, and through instruction" (Rogers, *Round Lake* D5) that, at least in regard to herbs, he must have received from his father or grandfather.

Jenness (60) distinguished three kinds of shamans using quite different methods in eastern Ontario: "*Wabeno*: the healer and charm-maker; *Ojiskiu*: the conjurer [shaking-tent]; *Kusabindugeyu*: the seer." John-Paul would fit into the latter category, although he also practiced as a herbalist.

By the time John-Paul had reached middle age, the older members of the community who in his earlier years had sought his services were deceased, and the members of his community who had been brought up in the twentieth century had become oriented toward the dominant culture.

Furthermore, the Church, with the only imposing building in the area, and the schools deliberately oriented the people away from the traditional culture. A series of Roman Catholic priests not only denounced John-Paul to their congregation and forbade the people to go to him, but, in a travesty of traditional concepts of interpersonal behavior, went to his home to denounce him to his face. The priest was seen by the members of the reserve as an intermediary with white culture and, hence, highly influential on their subsistence—government payments of diverse sorts. It is possible that the developing fear of shamans as sorcerers also contributed to his isolation. In any case, John-Paul had considerably reduced contact of any type with his community. And the community became alienated as well from the traditional culture. From an autobiographical essay by Wilfrid Pelletier of a Manitoulin Island reserve, it is clear that until the revival of Native American religions in the latter part of the twentieth century, he had been ignorant of traditional culture.

In John-Paul's typology of "flight," the third type pertains far more to the mystic experience than to shamanism. He further described such a flight as traveling to and merging with God, a ball of light, and, while the first two types of flights are done for others, the third and highest is done for oneself (Johnson, personal communication). In other words, the shamanistic ascents of John-Paul, when he had lost his function, became individualistic, were not integrated into the cultural matrix, and were conceived in purely personal terms: the union with the ultimate of the mystic experience. (For a fuller account and analysis, see Paper, *The Spirits* chapter 5.)

I have not come across any reference to the mystic experience by a medium, but I have discussed the issue with You Meiling, a highly adept Chinese medium, who was the General Secretary of the Republic of China Association of Mediums (see Paper, "Mediums" and *Through the Earth*) in 1995 and 2001. You has had the mystic experience a couple of times, as well as related union experiences. She does not, however, consider them associated with, let alone similar to, her mediumistic experiences. As we shall see below, there is a long literary tradition of reference to the mystic experience in China, which invariably treats the mystic experience as relating to a worldview that is the alternative to social functioning. You is no different in this regard. But, more important, as a reflective, articulate, intelligent person socially and institutionally recognized as a master medium, her understanding, given no other examples, must stand as representative.

SOUTH ASIA

THE UPANISHADS

The Upanishads, as other South Asian texts, were transmitted as an oral literature for many centuries before they were written down. Created from perhaps twenty-eight hundred to twenty-four hundred years ago, they came to be understood as commentaries to the Vedas, although, as we shall see, in part, they were antithetical to the Vedas. The Vedas originally were the sacred, oral texts of a tradition that has come to be called Vedic religion, the religion of the Indo-European Aryans who invaded or migrated into South Asia some thirty-five hundred years ago and remain the primary sacred oral texts of Hinduism.

Vedic religion was based on sacrificial rituals performed by aristocratic, hereditary priests (*brahmins*) for the hereditary warrior-ruling caste (*ksatriyas*). Once the Aryans had become the rulers of the northern part of South Asia, having shifted from a herding economy to an agricultural one, some began to shift their religious focus from the all-important sacrifices—necessary not only for kingship and all the necessities of life, but for the continuation of the cosmos itself—to personal, ecstatic religious experiences.

In a section of the *Chāndogya Upanishad* (5.3.–5.10), a king (*ksatriya*) reluctantly imparts a teaching regarding the spiritual life to a priest (*brahmin*): ". . . this knowledge has never yet come to Brahmans before you; and therefore in all the worlds has the rule belonged to the Kshatriya only" (all translations from the Upanishads are from Hume, slightly modified). This teaching is that there are two paths to live. One is that of the good person who fulfills his duty and performs the sacrificial rituals; this path leads to transmigration (*samsāra*). The second path is that of a life of meditation in the forest; succeeding on this path leads to liberation (*moksha*) from transmigration. A premise to all of this is the nature of life itself. *Samsāra* is a view of life modeled on the cycle of vegetation. Life repeats itself over and over again; the spiritual goal is to leave the cycle entirely—not to continue individual life (*ātman*), but to end it by merging with the all (*brahma*).

Although this interpretation is not absolutely compelling to all scholars, those who have had the mystic experience readily find in the statements of the Upanishads that the ultimate experience is the mystic experience in and of itself. First, there are explicit statements of the light common to the experience:

In the highest golden sheath
Is Brahma, without stain, without parts.
Brilliant is It, the light of lights—
That which knowers of the Ātman do know!
The sun shines not there, nor the moon and stars;
These lightnings shine not, much less this [earthly] fire!
After Him, as He shines, doth everything shine.
This whole world is illumined with His light.
Brahma, indeed, is this immortal. Brahma before,
Brahma behind, to right and to left.
Stretched forth below and above,
Brahma, indeed, is this whole world, this widest extent.

(Mundaka Upanishad 2.2.9–11)

Now, he who, without stopping the respiration, goes aloft
and who, moving about, yet unmoving, dispels darkness—he is
the Ātman. . . . For thus it has been said: "Now that serene one
who, rising up out of this body, reaches the highest light and
appears with his own form—he is the Ātman. . . . That is the
immortal, the fearless. That is Brahma." (*Maitri Upanishad* 2.2)

There are, assuredly, two forms of Brahma: the formed and
the formless: Now, that which is the formed is unreal; that which
is the formless is real, is Brahma, is light. (*Maitri Upanishad* 6.3)

In this experience, there is no sense perception, no thought; hence, of
course, the experience is ineffable:

There the eye goes not;
Speech goes not, nor the mind.
We know not, we understand not
How one could teach it.
Other, indeed, is It above the known,
And moreover above the unknown.
. . . . .
This indeed know as Brahma,
Not this that people worship as this.

(*Kena Upanishad* 3–4)

For someone raised in a worldview in which life is imperishable, continuing life after life a myriad of times, the experience is one in which the individual life (*ātman*) literally disappears into the timeless entirety of everything (*brahma*). The conclusion is that *samsāra* (the continual cycle of life) not only comes to an end; it never was. The understanding of *samsāra* is that it is but *māyā* (illusion). Only Brahma is real:

> This [*ātman*], verily, is That [*brahma*]. This, indeed, was That, even the Real. He who knows that wonderful being (*yaksha*) as the first-born—namely, that Brahma is the Real—conquers these worlds. Would he be conquered who knows thus that the great spirit as the first-born—namely, that Brahma is the Real? [No!] for indeed, Brahma is the Real. (*Brihad-Āranyaka Upanishad* 4)

And Brahma is who we really are:

> When cease the five
> [Sense-]knowledges, together with the mind (*manas*),
> And the intellect stirs not—
> That, they say, is the highest course.
> . . . . .
> Not by speech, not by mind,
> Not by sight can He be apprehended.
> How can He be comprehended
> Otherwise than by saying "He is" [*asti*]?
> He can indeed be comprehended by the thought "He is"
> And by [admitting] the real nature of both [his comprehensibility
>   and incomprehensibility].
> When he has been comprehended by the thought "He is"
> His real nature manifests itself.
> When are liberated all
> The desires that lodge in one's heart
> Then a mortal becomes immortal!
> Therein he reaches Brahma!
>
> (*Katha Upanishad* 6.10–14)

To attain the experience of *ātman* or *brahma*, the two being one and the same, is beyond instruction; it happens:

This Ātman is not to be obtained by instruction,
Nor by intellect, nor by much learning.
He is to be obtained only by the one whom he chooses;
To such a one that Ātman reveals his own person (*tanūm svām*)
                                        (*Katha Upanishad* 2.23)

The experience is bliss, pure and simple:

This is it!—thus they recognize
The highest, indescribable happiness.
                                        (*Katha Upanishad* 5.14)

HINDUISM

A philosophy based upon and placing the highest value on a functionless null experience, an experience in which the self disappears, is not likely to be promoted in any culture, let alone for a long time, unless it can be assimilated to other values. The Upanishads and the Vedas were synthesized into a complex system of values and goals that has come to be known in Europe as Hinduism. The term itself—literally, the "-ism" of the Indus Valley—simply denotes that generalized religious gestalt of South Asia which has no other specific name, such as Buddhism or Jainism.

As this general religious complex developed, four goals of life were understood for the aristocracy: *dharma,* duty and the learning of one's duty (depending on one's inherited social role); *artha,* the skills necessary to rule a state; *kāma,* the pleasures of life, including sex; and *moksha,* liberation from *samsāra.* These goals were not to be taken on simultaneously, but in sequence. It was understood that there were four related stages of life, each lasting about twenty years: student, warrior, householder, and recluse. Thus the traditions of sacrificial rituals and social roles were synthesized. Only toward the end of life, if one lived to old age, when one was free of duty to society and family, was it proper to pursue the private goal of self-liberation and the mystic experience.

Given that *moksha* had become a recognized goal, in spite of Upanishadic statements that it could not be learned, a variety of techniques developed to enhance its occurrence. Thus, the many yogas developed. Yoga, generally misunderstood in the West as exercises for health, means any set of techniques that "yokes" (an English word which shares the same Indo-European root as "yoga"), harnesses, one's will. Anyone practicing a life of intense self-discipline, such as a professional classical musician, is, in effect practicing yoga. Linked to spiritual development, as the term usually is, yoga most commonly refers to disciplines for the purpose of attaining *moksha*.

For some, the drive to attain *moksha* was so intense that all the other ends of life became meaningless. Shankara (c. 788–820) became a celibate early in life. His writings express a monistic (absolute nonduality) understanding that became a major school of Hindu thought called Vedānta, and undoubtedly stemmed from his own mystic experience(s):

> Therefore both bondage [*samsāra*] and liberation [*moksha*] are fictions of ignorance. They are not in the Atman. The Atman is infinite, without parts, beyond action. It is serene, stainless, pure. How can one imagine duality in Brahman, which is entire like the ether, without a second, the supreme reality?
>
> There is neither birth nor death, neither bound nor aspiring soul, neither liberated soul nor seeker after liberation—this is the ultimate and absolute truth. (Shankara 115)

BUDDHISM

Buddhism is unique among the major, in the sense of the number of adherents, religions. It is, along with Islam, but one of the two major religions that fits the modern popular notion that religions have founders; that is, they are started by a specific individual. And it is the only religion that fits the model of the mystic experience being the basis of religion, as found among some psychologists or psychiatrists as, for example, R. D. Laing (95): "Certain transcendental experiences seem to me to be the original wellspring of all religions." Theologically oriented historians of religions, in contrast, often understand mysticism from an evolutionary perspective: "Mysticism is a definite state in the historical development of religion and makes its appearance under certain well-defined conditions" (Scholem, *Major Trends* 7).

Toward the end of the period in which the Upanishads were created, historians of South Asia generally agree that there was a person with the common name of Gautama of the aristocratic Shakya clan living in the northeastern part of the Indian subcontinent twenty-five hundred years ago. As a relatively young man he literally abandoned his wife and child, as well as his clan obligations and sociopolitical roles, for a life of asceticism. For years he tried the various strategies then current to attain *moksha*, none being successful for him. Finally, while quietly sitting, he had what I assume from the early Buddhist teachings can only be understood as the mystic experience.

He then apprised his fellow seekers of his experience and recommended what came to be called the Middle Path, a practice that avoided both the life of a normal householder and extreme asceticism. He also suggested that seekers, instead of living in isolation, band together into a mutual, self-help brotherhood with fixed rules, thus inventing monasticism. Known as the Buddha, one who was enlightened by his experience, he must have been quite charismatic, as the religion he founded in his own lifetime continues to this day. His preaching was simple, based on what came to be called the Four Noble Truths: 1) *Samsāra* is essentially a continuous cycle of suffering (birth, sickness, old age, and death); 2) it is caused by desire (essentially the craving to exist in and of itself); 3) desires can be overcome; 4) overcome by following the way of the brotherhood (later modified for laypersons), the "eightfold path." The common South Asian cultural understanding of life as *samsāra* is the essential premise to these teachings.

In one of the early sutras (religious teachings understood to be essentially true), the Buddha is asked typical questions addressed to one who is understood to have experienced ultimate truth. He refuses to answer any of them, as they are all irrelevant to the existential crisis, *samsāra*:

> Accordingly, Mālunkyāputta, bear always in mind what it is I have not elucidated, and what it is that I have elucidated. . . . I have not elucidated, Mālunkyāputta, that the world is eternal; I have not elucidated that the world is not eternal [etc.]. . . . And why, Mālunkyāputta, have I not elucidated this? Because, Mālunkyāputta, this profits not nor has to do with the fundamentals of religion, nor tends to aversion, absence of passion, cessation, quiescence, the supernatural faculties, supreme wisdom and Nirvana; therefore have I not elucidated it.
>
> And what, Mālunkyāputta, have I elucidated? Misery, Mālunkyāputta, have I elucidated; the origin of misery have I elucidated; the cessation of misery have I elucidated; and the path leading to cessation of misery have I elucidated. . . . (*Majjihima-Nikāya*, Sutta 65 in Warren 122)

The goal of the path is the opposite of *samsāra*: *nirvāna*. And what is *nirvāna*? The Buddha refused to say; it is ineffable. We exist, we are in *samsāra*, essentially because we are ignorant. If we were not ignorant, then we would be in *nirvāna* and ipso facto understand it. Being ignorant, we cannot possibly understand it:

> Thus does this entire aggregation of misery exist. But on the complete fading out and cessation of ignorance ceases karma [leading to a chain of causation, ending with] on the cessation of birth, cease old age and death, sorrow, lamentation, misery, grief, and despair. Thus does this entire aggregation of misery exit. (*Mahā-Vagga* in Warren 83)

And what constitutes the core of our ignorance? It is the very understanding that we actually exist:

> He grasps the fourfold emptiness disclosed in the words: "I am nowhere a somewhatness for any one, and nowhere for me is there a somewhatness of any one." (*Visuddhi-Magga* in Warren 145)

Essentially nothing actually exists, including our selves:

> . . . the correct view in the light of the highest knowledge is as follows: "This is not mine; this am I not; this is not my Ego." (*Mahā-Vagga* in Warren 147)

That essentially neither I nor you exist is so fundamental to the basic, core Buddhist understanding that early Buddhism disagreed with the concept found in the Upanishads that became foundational to Hinduism. Buddhism denied actuality to the *ātman*, that there was anything whatsoever that existed with regard to the self.

It is to these two interconnected features, ineffability and the loss of self, that lead me to the assumption that the Buddha was articulating what he understood to be the lessons to be derived from the mystic experience. The Upanishads tend to put the experience in the terms of union, that the *ātman* and *brahma* are one and the same, a ineffable unity in which there is no self. Buddhism is but focusing on the nothingness aspect of the same experience, that the person's self disappears into the nullity of things as does everything else. These are simply two ways of relating to the blissful, ineffable null/union experience.

In this regard, a practical question arises given the fact of the success of Buddhism. How could a religion develop based on providing monks what were hoped to be effective means to have the mystic experience? (Nuns were later allowed, with the understanding that they would have to be re-born a monk in order to achieve enlightenment; South Asian Buddhism re-mains highly androcentric, and, until quite recently, nuns had disappeared.) Monks cannot survive without lay supporters; indeed, there must be far more lay supporters than monks. What could Buddhism offer to the masses? Gautama Buddha is hardly a role model for a husband, father, and ruler.

As pointed out in the previous section, Vedic religion was based on hereditary priests performing sacrificial rituals for hereditary warrior-rulers. When Buddhism began, there was a growing class of wealthy mer-chants that had no role in Vedic religion. Buddhism not only denied the existence of a self but the corresponding reality of castes or hereditary classes. South Asia has a monsoon season, a period of time when it inces-santly rains heavily. The monks needed shelter at this time. It seems that the merchants built monasteries and otherwise supported the monks and nuns in return for priestly services they were not receiving from the *brah-mins*. This is probably how the concept of lay-Buddhists, who followed considerably simpler rules than the monks, developed. The monks and nuns provided priestly, health, and teaching services in return for food, shelter, and other basic necessities. Thus, a practice founded on attaining an ecstatic null experience became the basis for a religion with similar so-cial and ritual roles to any other.

As the centuries passed, Buddhism became highly institutionalized and competed with other developing religious traditions for adherents and sup-port, state and otherwise. The doctrines became highly elaborate, schisms developed, and there arose a number of different subtraditions. Yet through all of these complex developments, Buddhism never lost its focus on the core experience. With the development of Mahayana, as a major split in inter-pretation, the emptiness of what we assume to be reality remained the key to *nirvāna*:

> And someone who discerns dharmas as in their own-being like
>   an illusion or a dream,
> Without a core, like a plantain tree, or similar to an echo,
> And who knows that the triple world, without exception, has
>   such an own-being,
> And is neither bound nor free, he does not discern Nirvana (as
>   separate from the triple world).

> He knows that all dharmas [the infinitely small, infinitely short
> in duration constituents of all that exists] are the same,
> empty, essentially without multiplicity.
> . . . . .
> All dharmas are the same, all the same, always quite the same.
> When one has recognized this, one understands Nirvana, the
> deathless and blest.
> (*Saddharmapundarīka in Conze, Buddhist Texts* 127)

Even the most elaborate of the philosophical texts, the *Mādhyamika Prajñāpāramitā [Perfect Wisdom]* sutras, focus on *śūnyatā* (emptiness):

> The Lord: On the seventh stage a Bodhisattva (Wisdom-being)
> does not seize on a self, or a being, or a soul, or a person, because,
> absolutely, a self, being, soul or person does not exist. (Conze,
> *Selected Sayings* 75)

Since nothing whatsoever actually exists, *samsāra* is an illusion, as is its opposite, *nirvāna*. Samsāra and *nirvāna* are one and the same; they are both empty; it is but a matter of experience, the mystic experience. And as this experience is available to anyone; all are potential Buddhas.

Buddhism has a tendency to summarize its doctrines in various lists, which can readily highlight the goals of Buddhist meditation. The "3 Doors to Deliverance" are "emptiness" (*śūnyatā*), "signlessness," and "wishlessness." The "8 Deliverances" are stages in order of deliverance:

1. Having form, he sees forms
2. not perceiving inward form he sees outward form
3. he becomes resolved on what is lovely
4. the station of endless space
5. the station of infinite consciousness
6. the station of nothing whatever
7. the station of neither perception nor nonperception
8. the cessation of perception and feeling. (Conze, "Lists")

(There is even a list of "18 Kinds of Emptiness.") Again, many of those who have had the mystic experience will readily recognize the above sequence of eight "deliverances."

The result of institutionalization has led, as with similar religious traditions, to an understanding that only those within not just Buddhism but the preferred sect of Buddhism, and only males, can achieve such an experience. Only those within the institution and having had the proper initiations can understand even the fundamental teachings. When I was carrying out the research for this section, I sought to speak with monk-scholar specialists on Buddhist meditation and psychology at the Buddhist universities in Taiwan. Even though I had lectured at these institutions in the past by invitation, save for an elderly monk-scholar who was a very close, old friend, no one would discuss these topics with me from a comparative perspective.

None of the above is particularly relevant to most Buddhists, who are neither monks nor nuns. In part, because Buddhism denied caste, the religio-social basis of Hindu culture, Buddhism did not undergo a resurgence as did Hinduism following the impact of Islam. Theravada Buddhism remains the dominant tradition in Sri Lanka and Southeast Asia west of Vietnam, and Pure Land Buddhism and Chan (Zen) remain important adjuncts of Chinese (and Japanese, Korean, Vietnamese) religion throughout East Asia. In the Theravadin area, Buddhism provides foci for worship, the predominant mode of religious behavior for laypersons, incorporating many aspects of the prior indigenous traditions. In China, Buddhism primarily provides supplementary mortuary rituals and a pleasant abode for the dead; rituals oriented toward the family dead being the central feature of Chinese religion. But in India, Buddhism is not a viable, living tradition, save for visitors from Japan and elsewhere oriented toward differing modes of Buddhism.

CHINESE RELIGION

The second oldest extant descriptions of the mystic experience, aside from the oblique early Buddhist statements, are from China of about twenty-four hundred years ago. They are contained within a text called the *Zhuangzi*, the early strata probably written by a person named Zhuang Zhou. The version that has come down to us was edited into its present form over six centuries after the earliest of the three strata was written. The text is quite eclectic, including many highly amusing didactic anecdotes.

All of the translations from this text are my own, and some will differ from standard translations (this section is extracted from Paper, *The Spirits* chapters 6 and 7). This is due to an inherent problem with regard to the translation of texts pertinent to ecstatic religious experiences. A. C. Graham ("Chuang-tzu and" 62, 71), whose translations of various sections are, on the whole, probably the best, has written that "Much of *Chuang-tzu* [Zhuangzi] is unintelligible at the present state of research." Furthermore, "Chuang-tzu is a mystical writer, and presents those who like myself are not mystics with the problem that often the choice of Chinese words is determined by a kind of experience which we have never shared."

Having had these experiences, to the contrary, I found those particular passages in the *Zhuangzi* crystal clear, indeed the most lucid in the text, and this is reflected in my translations.

To begin, there are a few references to the ecstatic experience of light. It is said of "The Spiritual Person" (Chap. 12:32/76; reference numbers are to *A Concordance*), ". . . his/her spirit ascends mounted on light with her/his bodily form extinguished." In an earlier section of the same chapter (17/41), there is related how a person with the talent to become a sage was taught the method to become a sage. One stage of this process involves becoming as the bright dawn (17/41, following the commentary of Cheng Xianying).

At the time the earliest strata of the *Zhuangzi* was being written, concepts were developing in regard to the nature of the Perfect Person, who is understood to be more advanced than one who is simply capable of shamanistic ascent, which was probably an anachronistic notion by the time of Zhuang Zhou. In the first chapter of the *Zhuangzi*, mention is made of a [trance-] "flight" by Liezi (see Graham, "The Date") that is considered inferior to ". . . mounting the regularity of Sky and Earth, riding the changes of the elemental forces, to wander in infinity. . . ." By itself, this statement is most ambiguous and has elicited extensive commentary. This passage is followed by a concluding explanation that seems to be a later addition (2/21–22): "Therefore, it is said, the Perfect Person is without self (*wuji*) . . ." (followed by two other characteristics). Hence, the passage in its entirety could be interpreted as saying that the egoless state, the mystic experience, is superior to shamanistic trance-flight. Such an interpretation would be most tenuous were it not supported by other passages.

Chapter 2 (3/1–3; Graham, "Chuang-tzu's Essay" 150) begins with a passage describing a person in a trance state: "Nanguo Zichi sat leaning on his armrest, looking up at the sky and breathing serenely, as though his self had lost its facade." His disciple on asking what was happening received the reply: "Just now, I had lost myself (*wu sang wo*). . . ." Although such a statement could imply a simple revery, the explanation which immediately follows as well as other passages lead to the conclusion that the egoless state is meant. In the first dialogue of chapter 4 (9/26–27), Kongzi (Confucius—it is not to be understood that Kongzi actually said anything like this) explains to his favorite disciple, Yen Hui, what he means by "fasting the mind":

Unify the will. Do not listen with the ears, listen with your mind; [rather] do not listen with your mind, listen with your essence [or spirit, *qi*]. Hearing stops at the ears; the mind stops at what tallies with it; essence being empty, awaits everything. Only the Dao gathers in emptiness, the fasting of the mind is [this] emptiness.

The relationship between Yen Hui and Kongzi is reversed in a brief dialogue in chapter 6 (19/93–94), where we have an equation of the egoless state and identity with the absolute. Yen Hui explains to Kongzi what he means by "sitting in forgetfulness" (*zuo wang*): "I allow my limbs and body to fall away, expel my intellectual faculties, leave my substance (*xing*), get rid of knowledge and become identical with the Great Universality (*da tong*); this is sitting in forgetfulness." In the last chapter of the early strata, we find a parallel concept (20/10–11), "The Nameless Man said: 'Let your/ Mind roam in vapidity/ Essence unite with the vastness. . . .'" In a following anecdote, Liezi brings a *shenwu* (a spirituality professional) who specializes in prognostication to visit his master. Each time his master entered a different trance state, leading to the *shenwu* on the fourth occurrence fleeing in terror. Perhaps what is meant is that Liezi's master was having the mystic experience and the *shenwu*, on "reading" his mind, was plunged into the void. Liezi then realizes he had never learned anything, returns home and lives in utmost, undifferentiated simplicity, "united in this way to the end of his life" (20/11–21/31).

In the early strata of the *Zhuangzi*, the references to the mystic experience emphasize the effects of the experience on one's understanding of reality and the corresponding essential meaninglessness of elite life patterns and preoccupations, leading to stressing the simple life. Concluding statements of the relationship of this knowledge to governing written in a different style have the flavor of having been added at a later date. The references to the mystic experience in the middle part of the *Zhuangzi*, written a century later, all seem to be a later development on these initial statements in that they relate the understanding gained from the experience to the primary intellectual concerns of the period, that is, governing and the growing interest in longevity (chap. 11–15), or are fully developed statements regarding the experience (chap. 21). One exception is in chapter 17 (43/27–28), in which a seemingly earlier saying is quoted: "I have heard it said: 'The Man of Dao is not heard of/ Perfect Power is not attained/ The Great Man Lacks self.'" (The saying apparently contains a play on words—"power" [*de*] and "attainment" are homophones in Chinese; the statement means "perfect power" comes of itself.)

The above statement is fully explained in a section of chapter 21 (55/24–56/38) where Kongzi receives instruction from Lao Dan (the reputed author of the *Daodejing*, edited in the same time period as the second strata of the *Zhuangzi*). Kongzi comes upon Lao Dan who, having bathed and spread his hair to dry, which could refer to a purification rite preparatory to shamanistic trance (Chen), is in an ecstatic state seemingly similar to the one referred to in the previously mentioned anecdote of chapter 2:

> Kongzi says, ". . . sir, just before your form and body were as still as a dead tree; it seemed that you had forgotten things, had left humankind and were standing utterly alone." Lao Dan responded, "My mind was roaming in the beginning of things [the Dao]."

Kongzi asks what he means and Lao Dan responds that the experience is ineffable, but he will try to explain it anyway. He does so in the context of Chinese cosmology of the period (see Paper, "Early Development"), in the interrelationships of Yin and Yang, Sky and Earth, and their transformations. To have the experience is to be the Perfect Person. Kongzi asks about the means to attain it. Within his answer, Lao Dan says, ". . . in the world, the myriad things are one. If you can attain this oneness and become identical with it. . . ." Kongzi says it must require much cultivating the mind to attain. Lao Dan's response is similar to the view of Bharati (65, 175), writing as a mystic:

> The zero-experience comes to those to whom it comes regardless of what they do. . . . There is really no predictable link between anything they [orthodox practitioners of yoga] or anyone else does and the occurrence or recurrence of the zero-experience.

For Lao Dan says:

> Water flows, not because it does anything, but because it is a natural talent. The power (*de*) of the Perfect Person [is the same]; he/she does not cultivate it, and yet she/he is unable to separate herself from all things. As the sky is naturally high, earth is naturally substantial, and the sun and moon are naturally bright, how can it (*de*) be cultivated?

This understanding of the mystic experience, that it comes not from trying, but rather from ceasing to try for it, if one has a nature (talent) suited to it, is reiterated in a passage in the late, last chapter (33:93/56–57) that has the appearance of being a quotation from an older work no longer extant:

> Barrier Keeper Yin said: "Where self is without an abode,/ Things of themselves will manifest their forms [to the person]./ His/her movements, like water;/ Her/his stillness, like a mirror;/ His/her response, like an echo./ . . . / In union with it, she/he is harmonious;/ [If he/she tries to] attain it, it will slip away./ . . ."

The mystic experience can lead to a questioning if not rejection of social and cultural norms, since it provides a reality other than that provided by language and acculturation, except in cultures where the experience has been incorporated into the core ideology. When interpreted, the experience comes to be understood through and related to the culture of the experiencer, but would still lack social value and, hence, not receive reification.

In the early strata of the *Zhuangzi*, those parts that treat the mystic experience indicate the experience leads to a rejection of the traditional or developing roles of the elite, to the adoption of a rustic existence (without, one assumes, the burdens of the peasant). This interpretation, being socially afunctional, would have little appeal except to those who had or were inclined toward the experience. For such concepts to survive, and for us to be aware of them more than two millennia later, they would have had to been integrated into the cultural system and come to be seen as having positive rather than negative value, as occurred with Buddhism and Hinduism discussed earlier.

In the development of the *Zhuangzi* we see the same process taking place. In the middle strata, as previously mentioned, most of the sections that directly or indirectly refer to the mystic experience do so in the context of elite concerns of twenty-three hundred years ago, a century after the writing of the first strata of the text. Hence, the earlier sections came to be interpreted differently than perhaps was the intention of the original author. It is probably because the middle section dealt with these concerns—governing and longevity—that the *Zhuangzi* survived.

In chapter 11, we find a section relating the mystic experience to the developing interest in longevity, an interest that later became one of the central concerns of Daoism. In a dialogue (27/39) between the Yellow Emperor (a mythic ruler/culture hero) and a master who lived on Emptiness and Identity (as a place), the Yellow Emperor learns to renounce active governing and turn toward the Dao of Perfection. In this discourse, the master says: "I maintain this unity in order to abide in this harmony; therefore, I have been able to cultivate my body for twelve hundred years and my form has never become feeble."

The mystic experience does have the effect of rendering death (or *saṃsāra* in the case of Buddhism) meaningless, as can be found in Alfred, Lord Tennyson's self-report of a mystic experience:

> . . . individuality itself seemed to dissolve and fade away into boundless being, and this not a confused state but the clearest, the surest of surest, utterly beyond words—where death was an almost laughable impossibility. . . . (cited in William James, 295)

For those reading interpretations of the experience in a culture that values long life, it is quite understandable that the experience came to be understood to actually cause the lengthening of life. Hence, in a fifth-century text, the *Santian neijie jing*, we find:

> Thus Laozi ordered all men to meditate on the True, to collect the Tao [Dao], to harden and strengthen their root and origin. Thereby man [sic] should reach a state in which he never loses his original source of life and can live forever. (Cited in Kohn 132)

The zero-experience comes to be interpreted as not only having the function of promoting longevity, but more important to the dominant elite concerns of the time, to bring about truly effective governing. In a dialogue following the previously cited one (27/44–28/57), the experience is related to inactive governing (*wei wuwei*) in distinction to normal governing (*zhi*), which inevitably leads to disaster. Cloud Chief, who is followed as a leader in spite of his inclination not to lead, asks a master what to do. The master responds: "As a *xian*, as a *xian*, return [to the source]" (for the meaning of *xian*, see Paper, *The Spirits* chap. 3). Cloud Chief asks for instruction. The master responds with terminology identical to the previously translated statement of Yen Hui to Kongzi in chapter 6 of the text:

> You only need abide in inactivity (*wuwei*) and things will transform themselves. Allow your mind and body to fall away, spit out your intellectual faculties, forget you are like other things, and [become one with] the Great Unity (*da tong*) vast and deep.

Become thus and each of the myriad things will return to the root without being aware of it.

The term, Great Unity, later took on the meaning of political unity; currently, it is found in the anthem of Taiwan (Republic of China). It is clear, however, that the term refers to the mystic experience in the *Zhuangzi* from its context with the segment following (28/65–66), also concerning government: "[Join with] the Great Unity and become selfless."

The following four chapters (12–15) in parts utilize terminology and concepts derived from the mystic experience, sometimes toward and other places away from governing the world, from becoming a true king. A philosophical reinterpretation of the mystic experience, with perhaps the experience itself lost, seems to have taken place; that is, the mystic experience has been successfully integrated into the emerging elite culture as a novel approach to the dominant concern.

Indeed, with the development of institutional Daoism beginning in the late second century CE, not only did Laozi ("Old Master" or Lao Dan), the metaphorically named reputed author of the *Daodejing*, become divinized (see Seidel), but even earlier so did one of the terms for the mystic experience, *taiyi* (Great Singleness): "The Great One as a personified god has been commonly venerated as an astral deity in the official cult ever since the Han dynasty" (Kohn 134).

A further integration of the mystic experience in traditional elite and semi-elite cultures took place in the following centuries. The subject is moot for the common people because while mystic experiences undoubtedly occur among ordinary Chinese people, they are unlikely to be in a socioeconomic circumstance that would allow for the valuing of nonfunctional ecstasy. In any case, as the literary and elite traditions were coterminous, we cannot expect anything to be recorded of these publicly unspectacular experiences among the nonelite, in contrast to the many recorded stories of magicians and other wonder workers (see DeWoskin).

The introduction of Buddhism and the development of institutional Daoism enhanced the interest of the Chinese elite in meditation and related practices. However, these practices were not necessarily oriented toward attaining the mystic experience. The focus of the remainder of this section will be limited to the mystic experience in its relationship to the avocations of the elite. I have concluded that the mystic and other ecstatic religious experiences were a major stimulus to the primary pastimes of the traditional elite: aesthetic activity. As well, aesthetic expression was the solution to a problem found in all cultures: how to express the ineffable mystic experience.

The traditional Chinese elite were males (only males were eligible to take the civil service examinations, the only recognized and legitimate means for obtaining elite status, socially acceptable wealth, and political power) who were highly accomplished in *wen*, in all its multiple meanings: the corpus of received literature, the creation of literature, writing as an art, clan and state rituals; in other words, all the constituents of being "civilized" from the standpoint of the dominant class. There were four theoretical occupations (two root: scholar-official, farmer; and two branch: artisan and merchant) but only two officially recognized classes: scholar-officials and all others (excepting the imperial family who were above all such distinctions). In actuality, merchants vied with the scholar-officials for power and status.

A millennium and a half of power struggles (among scholar-officials, the military, merchants, court eunuchs, and the hereditary aristocracy) were ultimately won by the scholars, who wore distinctive garb and had a special, legal status, with the full development of the civil service system by the eleventh century. Wealthy merchants were co-opted into the system by being allowed to purchase civil service ranks at a price that reduced their economic power. Contemporary scholarship has expanded this view to include a somewhat differently educated middle class of middling-wealthy merchants, professionals (physicians, etc.), and government clerks, who were often oriented toward Daoism and formed poetry and calligraphy circles.

The *wenren* (*wen*: literature/writing/culture-person) or literati, the traditional elite, stood between two opposite ideals: *ren* and *ziran*. *Ren* (etymology: person and two), usually translated as "benevolence," means the ultimate in social responsibility. *Ren* was the ideal of the *rujia* (usually but incorrectly translated as "Confucianism" and *ru* alone as "scholar"), the dominant ideology of state and clan religion combined, as interpreted by Kongzi and those who nominally followed him. *Ziran* (literally: "of itself," "spontaneity") expresses both the ideal of nature (as opposed to human artifice) and individuality or personal freedom. *Ziran* is a basic tenet of *daojia* (usually translated as "Daoism" but nonetheless distinct from *daojiao*—Daoist religious institutions per se—albeit the two are considerably interrelated).

The concept of *ziran* may well have arisen from an interpretation of the mystic experience. As one emerges from the mystic experience trance, one first is simply aware of being aware, from nothingness there is now a somethingness. At first this somethingness is diffused, undistinguished, but as consciousness increasingly returns, we begin to discriminate what we see into objects with remembered names and meanings, and we distinguish ourselves as a distinct entity as well. In classic Daoist metaphysics, creation is understood to be an ongoing, spontaneous happening. Everything, including each of us, continually creates itself. In formal terms: initially there is nothingness (*wu*), from this there arises a somethingness (*you*). To give it a name, we call it the "Dao." At first singular, it begins a process of discrimination. From the one, the Dao, we have two—Sky and Earth with regard to matter, Yin and Yang with regard to energy. And from the two are produced or created the myriad things. As this cosmogonic scheme but replicates the end of the mystic experience, and given the relationship of the experience to Daoist thought, I can but assume that the scheme arises from cogitation on the experience. Hence, *ziran* is an understanding of creation, nature, the world, and ourselves from the standpoint of the experience of "nothingness," of "loss of self," of "sitting in forgetfulness."

A *wenren* could express his individuality in many ways, including modes of living, but usually did so as a *wenren*, that is with his brush, the basic *wen* implement of poetry, calligraphy, and painting. Where a *wenren* could be found between the two polar ideals of *ren* and *ziran* depended on both circumstances and personal inclinations but rarely would be exclusively one or the other.

For over a millennium, poetry, calligraphy, and painting have been considered by the elite as the Three Incomparables (*sanjue*). Together with music of the *qin*, they comprise the traditional Chinese elite aesthetic activities, and they are very much involved with the mystic experience.

The earliest known Chinese poet is Qu Yuan (fourth century CE). His poetry established a poetic style that was highly influential on the development of Chinese poetry. Some of his poems and those of a similar style, written in a later period when Daoist thought had spread among the intelligentsia, emphasized the mystic experience:

> When I looked, my startled eyes saw nothing;
> When I listened, no sound met my amazed ear.
> Transcending Inaction, I came to Purity,
> And entered the neighborhood of the Great Beginning.
>   (Last lines of "Yuan you," Hawkes 87)

The poem that perhaps best captures the ineffable is by Tao Qian (365–427). This is not only my own view, but that of Chinese culture in general. We have little hard data for the life of Tao Qian. The traditional biographies are apocryphal and dwell on his legendary aspects. However, they do coincide with his autobiographical essay—"I have lived alone in

my poor house, drinking wine and writing poetry" (Hightower, *The Poetry*
58)—and his poetry. Rejecting office, the only source of wealth available
to a member of his class, and lacking a large inheritance, to a degree, he
lived as a farmer. Tao took pleasure, perhaps even focused his life, on
drinking and writing poetry, and he came to represent for subsequent generations the alternative lifestyle to the dominant imperatives—to serve
family, clan, and state. His image is that of the semirecluse having like-
minded companions, living a simple life close to nature (interpreted in
various ways).

For Tao, wine was perhaps not so much an escape from reality (it was
certainly used as an excuse to avoid offers of government positions, an inherently dangerous occupation during his time) but an escape to another reality
(alternate state of consciousness), and poetry was the means of expressing it.
But it is also an example, found in, for example, Sufi poetry, of using alcoholic
inebriation as a metaphor for the mystic experience. Poem number five of the
series "Twenty Poems after Drinking Wine" is often cited as a classic example
of a unitive, if not mystic, experience achieved through nature and expressed
via poetry (Chang 190–91):

> I built my hut besides a traveled road
> Yet hear no noise of passing carts and horses.
> You would like to know how it is done?
> With the mind detached, one's place becomes remote.
> Picking chrysanthemums by the eastern hedge
> I catch sight of distant South Mountain [Mount Lu]:
> The mountain air is lovely as the sun sets
> And flocks of flying birds return together.
> In these things there is a fundamental truth
> I would like to tell, but there are no words.
>   (modifying Hightower, *The Poetry* 30)

Thus the ineffable is communicated through paradox aesthetically expressed,
for "no words" are still words.

As with most early civilizations, writing was a characteristic of the
earliest Chinese civilization, over three and a half millennia in the past.
Less typical was a major use: the means for communicating with super-
normal powers. When well over two millennium in the past, the warrior-
priest clansmen who comprised the elite instead became semimilitary

protobureaucrats, they remained ritual specialists. Writing (*wen*) then took precedence over military skills (*wu*) and maintained a sacred aura as well.

With improvements in brush and ink and the development of paper, the style of writing became more fluid, allowing many minor variations, hence, writing itself became more personal, and calligraphy came to be understood as the aesthetic mode par excellence. Calligraphy, in which all the elite, the scholar-officials, were adept to some degree, began to serve as a complementary but opposite activity to those of the official realm: the spontaneity (*ziran*) of Daoist thought and later, Chan Buddhism, reflected in free-flowing calligraphy divorced from conscious thought, as opposed to the ritual order (*li*) of official life reflected in formal styles of calligraphy.

The extremes of spontaneity to which calligraphy could be carried in Chan Buddhism is exemplified by the "Mad *caoshu*" of the Monk Huaisu (725–85), as described in the poem attributed to Li Bo (701–62), China's best-known poet:

> The Master high on wine, sits in his rope-chair
> in an instant he has covered thousands of sheets:
> the room is filled with whirlwinds and driving
> rains, falling flowers and flying snowflakes!
> He stands, goes over to the wall, with a single sweep
> he brushes a line of words as big as dippers!
> We hear the voices of gods and demons.
>
> (Chaves 212)

This poem may well refer to a practice in which a brush laden with ink is placed in the hand of a Chan monk just coming out of trance.

Poetry and calligraphy were the stock-in-trade of the elite (both were tested in the civil service examinations); only certain aspects of each furnished an alternative to official activity and concepts. Painting became an important elite activity only considerably later and remained an avocation.

Listed among the "Four Masters" of Song dynasty calligraphy, when literati aesthetics reached its full development, Su Shi (Dong-po, 1037–1101) was one of the major Chinese poets of all time, an important official (when not in political exile) who was leader of the conservative faction in Song politics, and an amateur painter. More than any other, Su Shi was responsible for the direction of literati aesthetics. Another literati artist described Su Shi's tendency at literary gatherings to fall asleep after several cups of wine, then awaken and rapidly paint (Lin 277); in Su Shi's own words:

> When my empty bowels receive wine, angular strokes come
>   forth,
> And my heart's criss-crossing give birth to bamboo and rock.
> What is about to be produced in abundance cannot be contained:
> It erupts on your snow-white wall.
>
> (Bush 35)

Su Shi explicitly relates the trance of self-loss to artistic activity in a poem on the painting of his close friend Wen Tung (d. 1079):

> When Yü-k'e [Wen Tong] paints bamboo
> He sees bamboo, not himself.
> Not only is he unaware of himself
> Trance-like he leaves his body.
> Body and soul once merged
> Endless freshness flows.
> Since Chuang [Zhuangzi] is no longer here
> Who else can know such absorption.
>
> (Stanley-Baker 14)

The *qin* was understood as a complement to the *sanjue*, the one literati aesthetic pursuit not directly connected to the brush. For the *qin* was a musical instrument almost exclusively played by the elite; its small sound box does not put forth a volume sufficient for concerts. By at least two millennia ago, playing the *qin* had religious connotations. According to the *Huainanzi* (second century BCE), the *qin* developed "in order to be able to return to the spiritual realm, to still the passions, and to turn back to one's heavenly mind/heart" (text in van Gulik 40; trans. my own). Many *qin* compositions were based on passages from the *Zhuangzi*; for example, "Liezi riding the wind."

Playing the *qin* was understood as a means for entering an ecstatic state, as well as a way of expressing the mystic experience through *ziran*. Toward the end of a sixteenth-century essay on the *qin*, we find:

> [In playing the *qin*,] if one's bearing is venerable, then one is able
> to deeply understand the Dao, one's spirit will merge with the

Dao. Accordingly, it is said, "Virtuous [playing] is not a matter of the hands but of the mind/heart; music is not a matter of sounds but of the Dao; producing music is not a matter of tones but of spontaneity/nature [*ziran*]. Thereby one may be stirred by the harmony of Sky and Earth; thereby one can merge with the essence [*de*] of the deities." (text in van Gulik 78; trans. my own)

6

Ethnohermeneutics II: West

The Western religious traditions, predominantly the Religions of the Book—Judaism, Christianity, and Islam—share a commonality that distinguishes them from all other religions: monotheism, in its various guises. The focus on a single deity, even if a Trinity, creates a predilection toward singularity. Hence, the ultimate and God must be identical; whereas, the ultimate and the deities are not the same in all other traditions.

For the dominant strands of the Religions of the Book, it would seem that an experience of identity with the ultimate would compromise a basic theological premise that God as Creator and humans as created must remain separate. This understanding would accordingly mandate a negative attitude toward an ecstatic experience of union. And while such attitudes do exist in these religious traditions, as will be seen in the following studies, in all there is at least a minority stream that values the mystic experience.

This chapter will be divided into five sections. The middle three sections encompass the Religions of the Book. The first section examines the most important influence on the mystical aspects of these traditions. A fifth section briefly discusses modern Western developments that ostensibly lie outside of these three traditions; that is, they are reputedly secular. Conclusions that can be drawn from these studies, as well as the contemporary situation in these regards, will be found in the final, concluding chapter.

PLOTINUS

A major influence on the interrelated medieval mystic traditions of Judaism, Christianity, and Islam that centered in Spain prior to the late fifteenth-century expulsion of non-Christians are the teachings of Plotinus (d. 270) as

found in the *Enneads*. The foremost mystic of the Hellenistic world, he relates
to the Religions of the Book in this regard as the Upanishads do to Hinduism. Plotinus was a professional philosopher who based his teachings on his
own "Union" experiences, which his disciple and biographer, Porphyry,
stated he had had four times; Porphyry himself had the experience once (see
Plotinus 17).

For Plotinus, the mystic experience was utterly ineffable: "Thus The
One is in truth beyond all statement" (*Enneads* V.3.13—all trans. by
MacKenna/Page). The experience can but be discussed from the standpoint
of what it is not; that is, by negation. We understand it not from the experience in and of itself, since it is a null experience, but from the aftermath
of the experience: "And we can and do state what it is not, while we are
silent as to what it is; we are, in fact, speaking of it in the light of its sequels;
unable to state it, we may still possess it" (V.2.14).

As we saw in Daoist approaches to the topic and as we will find in
Eckhart, Plotinus understands the ultimate to be a singular nothingness
from which all things which exist arise: "It is precisely because there is
nothing within the One that all things are from it" (V.1.1). While Plotinus
places this within a context of logic, that logic is an extension of the experience per se, for the experience of pure nullity is exactly that.

As in the *Zhuangzi* and Bharati, Plotinus understands that, although one
must prepare to receive the experience, there is no certainty that one will experience it; no preparation can guarantee its occurrence. But preparation allows us to "surrender" to the experience with a degree of understanding.
"We must not run after it. . . . This advent, still, is not by expectation: it is
coming without approach" (V.5.8).

This advent is put in terms of a vision, but this vision is not an actual
one, as it is purely of nonvisual light: "We may know we have had the vision when the Soul has suddenly taken light. This light is from the Supreme
and is the Supreme . . . the light is proof of the advent" (V.3.17). Some
modern commentators seem to understand that this "light" is metaphorical,
but those who have had the experience know that the statement is meant
literally. It is the light that precedes merging with nothingness, becoming
one with the "Supreme," with "God":

> The man formed by this mingling with the Supreme must—if
> he only remember—carry its image impressed upon him: he is
> become the Unity, nothing within him or without inducing
> any diversity; no movement now, no passion, no outlooking
> desire, once this ascent is achieved; reasoning is in abeyance and

all Intellection and even, to dare the word, the very self: caught away, filled with God, he has in perfect stillness attained isolation; all the being calmed, he turns neither to this side nor to that, not even inwards to himself; utterly resting he has become very rest. (VI.9.11)

As in all the examples of the experience discussed in this study, the mark of the mystic experience is finally the disappearance of self.

With Plotinus, we can use the term "mysticism" as an all-encompassing rubric for these and related experiences in the full Hellenistic sense of the word, relating to the necessity of an initiatory ecstatic experience for understanding. Thus the Hellenistic use of the term would include the mystic experience itself. For, in the end, the mystic experience can only be fully communicated to one who already has had the experience, and for such a person, the communication is unnecessary: "This is the purport of that rule of our Mysteries: 'Nothing Divulged to the Uninitiate': the Supreme is not to be made a common story, the holy things may not be uncovered to the stranger, to any that has not himself attained to see" (VI.9.11). Yet, paradoxically, Plotinus writes his book, and I write this one.

JUDAISM

Because of the understanding that the Creator and created are fundamentally different, there tends to be an understanding that self-loss and merging with the ultimate does not take place within Judaism in and of itself. The most influential modern scholar of Jewish mysticism, Gershom Scholem, promoted this view:

> . . . it is only in extremely rare cases that ecstasy signifies actual union with God, in which the individuality abandons itself to the rapture of complete submersion in the divine stream. Even in this ecstatic frame of mind, the Jewish mystic almost invariably retains a sense of the distance between the Creator and His creature. (*Major Trends* 122–23)

I have found a great reluctance among many contemporary scholars of Judaism to even think about this topic, let alone the general subject of ecstatic religious experience.

Scholem in his major work on Jewish mysticism, however, refers to a primordial nothingness that casts doubt on this assertion. He discusses a "mystical 'nothingness' from which all the other stages of God's unfolding in the Sefiroth [*sefirot*] emanate and which the Kabbalists call the highest Sefirah, or the 'supreme crown' of divinity." The womb of the first is "Nothing"; Nothing is pure absolute "Being." "In the Zohar, as well as in the Hebrew writings of Moses de Leon, the transformation of Nothing into Being is frequently explained by the use of one symbol, that of the primordial point" (*Major Trends* 217–18).

In all other traditions discussed in this study, this nothingness is not a theoretical, hypothetical concept, but it is one that is grounded in the explicit experience of the mystic experience and its aftermath, the creation of being from nothingness. It is most unlikely that Judaism is an exception and that concepts identical to those of other mystical traditions did not arise from the universal experience of self-loss.

The great difficulty in coming to terms with the Jewish understanding in this regard is that few Jewish mystics explicitly discuss their own experiences but tend to discuss their personal understanding within highly abstract constructs or to refer to the understandings of others. A few Jewish scholars have explicitly disagreed with the above assertion of Scholem and others, and this study will primarily be based on their research, particularly that of Moshe Idel and Elliot Wolfson. Their studies are based on medieval mystics, but there is a possible earlier reference.

MARIA THE HEBREW

The first known Western alchemist is known as Maria Hebraea, Maria the Hebrew. She lived no later than the early third century, possibly in Alexandria, which had a large Jewish community. Her own writings have not survived, but her work is known through extensive quotations in the writings of other alchemists living a few generations after her. While alchemy is at the base of modern chemistry, in itself it is first and foremost a spiritual practice whether found in China or the Hellenistic world.

All of Maria's quoted writings are specific to alchemy, but there is a passage that is reminiscent of Chinese thought that precedes her time. Given the linkage of this statement in China to the mystic experience, it raises a vague possibility with regard to her own understanding.

Christianos gives this statement ["One is the All, and it is through it that the All is born"] a more succinct form and says that Maria uttered it in an ecstatic shriek (*kraugazein*): "Therefore the Hebrew prophetess shrieked, 'One becomes two, two becomes three, and by means of the third and fourth achieves unity: thus two are but one.'" (Patai 65–66)

This statement is quite similar to those discussed in the section on China in the preceding chapter but, of course, it is open to an exclusively alchemical interpretation as well.

LIGHT

There are many discourses on mystic light in Judaism, one being that of Eleazor ben Judah of Worms (ca. 1165–1230) in his *Sha'are ha-Sod ha-Yihud we-ha-'Emmunah*:

> The Creator has no body, physical stature, image, or form at all. . . . The glory is in an appearance of the resplendent light, which is called *Shekhina*. . . . From the resplendent light He creates his Glory . . . the appearance of the vision is in the heart of one who sees. . . . (Wolfson 214)

This light is also the final experience when related to the Kabbalistic *sefirot*. In an anonymous thirteenth century commentary on the *sefirot*, probably written in Castile, we find the following:

> [In the final, tenth *sefirah*] Then your soul will don the garment of splendor and beauty, grace and love, and you will be crowned with the resplendent light that surrounds the Presence, and this is the secret in which is contained the mystery of the upper and lower knowledge. (Wolfson 284)

Wolfson reflects on this passage,

> The goal of gnosis of the sefirotic pleroma is the unitive experience with the Presence, the last of the ten emanations, which is here characterized as the donning of the garment and the wearing

of the crown of resplendent light. Time and again in kabbalistic texts, union with the *Shekhinah* is depicted in terms of this
imagery, especially the crown.

What is essential to emphasize in this context is that the
unitive experience results from a visual knowledge of the *sefirot*, a knowledge that scholars all too often consider merely
theoretical or discursive in nature. (Wolfson 284)

Different from contemporaneous Christian and Islamic discussions
of mystical experiences, the formative medieval Jewish authors of the
twelfth and thirteenth centuries tend to avoid descriptions of their own
experience. Hence, what seem to be theoretical discussions of Moses' and
Ezekiel's visions may actually reflect the authors' religious imagination, if
not, indeed, their actual experiences (Wolfson 331–32). Thus, the Jewish
mystics discussions of light need not be seen as metaphorical but actual,
and Wolfson himself, as quoted above, relates this experience to that
of unity.

UNITY, SELF-LOSS, AND NOTHINGNESS

Contrary to Scholem and the many scholars influenced by him with regard
to the lack of references to the mystic experience in Judaism as discussed
above, Moshe Idel has explicitly argued to the contrary: "I shall propose an
alternative view on expressions of *unio mystica* in Kabbalah: far from being
absent, unitive descriptions recur in Kabbalistic literature no less frequently
than in non-Jewish mystical writings" (Idel, *Kabbalah* 60).

One of the most explicit statements of unity can be found in the writings of Abraham Abulafia (124–91): ". . . he and He become one entity, in-
separable during this act" (Idel, *Kabbalah* 62). Abulafia influenced Isaac of
Acre, who wrote in *Ôzar Hayyim*:

[when the soul] cleaves to the Divine Intellect, and It will cleave
to her . . . and she and the intellect become one entity, as if some-
body pours out a jug of water into a running well, that all becomes one. And this is the secret meaning of the saying of our
sages: "Enoch is Metratron." (Idel, *The Mystical Experience* . . . 128)

Idel understands the above remark to have "originated in personal experience."

In post-medieval Hasidism, the experience of unity is understood to be the ultimate end of prayer. Shneir Zalman writes:

> And this is the true cleaving, as he becomes one substance with God into whom he was swallowed, without being separate [from him] to be considered as a distinct entity at all. This is the meaning [of the verse], "and you shall cleave to him"—to cleave, literally. (Idel, *Kabbalah* 71)

Union is definitely understood to mean loss or extinction of the self. In the writings of the Great Maggid, Rabbi Dov Baer of Mezherich, we find the following:

> And when he unites with God, who is the Alpha of the world, he becomes *'ADaM* . . . and man must separate himself from any corporeal things to such an extent that he will ascend through all the worlds and be in union with God, until [his] existence will be annihilated, and then he will be called *'ADaM*. (Idel, *Kabbalah* 65)

Similarly, Menahem Mendel of Vitebsk, in his *Sefer Peri HaArez*, writes,

> the nature of all recipients is that they are stupefied and this is the matter of their annihilations, since they self-annihilate themselves and they become comprised in the sources of (their) influx, and therefore this *tremendum* is [tantamount to] the complete *devekut*, since he [namely, the mystic] is comprised in *Eiyn Sof*, Blessed be He. (Idel, "Universalization" 40)

As in several other traditions discussed in this study, this self-extinction in union with the ultimate can be understood as a union with nothingness:

> As one contemplates that it is impossible to cleave to Him, blessed by He, through perception, then there arises an acknowledgment, that is, to be annihilated within Him, blessed be He, and to become naught from one's substance and from the substance of the worlds, in an acknowledgment that accepts that He cannot be comprehended, and that there is nothing besides Him. . . . (*Advodat ha-Levi*, Va-Yetse, 34a in Elior 183)

A disciple of the Great Maggid, Levi Isaac of Berdichev, writes in *Kedushat ha-Levi*,

> When the *Zaddik* cleaves to the nought, and is [then] annihilated, then alone he worships the Creator from the aspect of all the *Zaddikim*, since no division of the attributes is discernable there at all. . . . There is a *Zaddik* who cleaves to the nought and nevertheless returns afterward to his essence. (Elior 72)

In Jewish mysticism, it is not always understood that union with God is but a temporary experience. Hence, there are warnings against allowing oneself to be dissolved into nothingness due to an assumption that returning to the state of a separate existence is not a subsequent step. But clearly in the above passage, it is accepted that at least some do come back to their former separate being.

All of the above expressions and understandings are not only of the past but are part of a living tradition. The following statements are from the writings of a then young member of a Hasidic community, someone who understood the mystic experience not only from the traditional texts but from experience:

> The word *bitul* [self-abnegation] implies self-nullification, the suspension of oneself, one's own feelings and reactions in deference to the Divine will as codified in Jewish law. At a deeper level, it also refers to a meditative-mystical state of egolessness and absorption in the Divine. (Lefcoe 55)

> . . . the famous prophetic vision recounted in the first chapter of the book of Ezekiel, where the verse states: "And the living creatures were running and returning." In the Kabbalistic texts, the word for "living creatures," *chayot*, is re-vowalized and read as *chayut*, "life-force," with the interpretation being that the life force of all worlds is continuously "running" back into the G-dhead, and then "returning" back to enliven the world. (Lefcoe 62)

THE 'EIYN SOF

Given the varieties of technical language that developed within the diverse aspects of Jewish mysticism, one term, in an above quotation, came to represent the very essence of the mystic experience: *'Eiyn Sof* (*'Ein Sof*, *'en-sof*), the Infinite. By the emergence of the first recognizable Kabbalasti-tradition in thirteenth-century Gerona, a small Catalan city, the term had become the one that designated the ultimate of the mystic experience:

> *'En-sof* there [Gerona] is a technical, indeed artificial, term de-
> tached from all adverbial associations and serving as a noun desig-
> nating God in all his inconceivability . . . God as the Infinite. . . .
> (Scholem, *Origins* 431)

"'Ein Sof is, in the words of Azriel of Gerona, 'absolutely undifferentiated in a complete and changeless unity (*Perush 'Eser Sefirot*)'" (Ginsburg 25). The term, literally meaning "without end," refers to that which is essentially non-dual and signifies the unity of opposites.

It is with the later Hasidic movement that *'Eiyn Sof* gains common usage in this regard and represents the mystic experience in and of itself. The term becomes the single expression for the nonexistent essence into which we disappear, as found, for example, in the writings of Rabbi Yehiel Mikhael of Zlowczow, "one of the Besht's important disciples and a companion of the Great Maggid":

> . . . for the branch arrives at its root, this [arrival] being a union
> with the root, and the root is the *'Eiyn Sof*; thence the branch is
> also *'Eiyn Sof*, as its existence was annihilated as in the simile of
> the single drop which falls into the great sea, and arrived at its
> root, and hence is one with the water of the sea, so that it is to-
> tally impossible to recognize it per se. (Idel, *Kabbalah* 68)

The "root" is the all, the totality, the infinity; hence, the *'Eiyn Sof*, as in the writings of "one of the first masters of Hasidism," Rabbi Menahem Nahum of Chernobyl:

> . . . and he becomes attached to the divine unity by means of the
> union of the part to the all, which is *'Eiyn Sof*. Consequently,
> the light of the holiness of *'Eiyn Sof* shines in him, as the part
> cleaves to its root. (Idel, *Kabbalah* 66)

The term, furthermore, tends to be connected with light, indicating that the term is associated with the preliminary aspects of the mystic experience as well:

> . . . until we shall be able to receive the great brightness [and]
> cleave ourselves, gradually, to *'Eiyn Sof*, blessed by He, this being
> the core of the reward that we receive from the Creator. . . .
> (Rabbi Qalonimus Qalman Epstein in Idel, *Hasidism* 91)

As well, *'Eiyn Sof* is associated with Nothingness in the context of reflecting experience:

> . . . and they stir all the worlds to return to the aspects of the
> Nought, and then the unification is attained, since all the as-
> pects of unification and intercourse are an ascent to the aspect
> of *'Eiyn Sof*. And the world would be annihilated and would
> completely return to the Nought, to the aspect of *'Eiyn Sof*.
> (Rabbi Yizhag Aiziq Yehudah Yehiel Safrin of Komarno in
> Idel, *Hasidism* 130)

CONCLUDING REMARKS

In the main, the contemporary Jewish attitude toward mysticism, let
alone the mystic experience, is to ignore if not deny its relevance within
Judaism. Certain contemporary trends are softening that position, especially that of Kabbalah studies entering the New Age marketplace; the
growth of *baal teshuva* ("returnees") within Hasidism; and the Renewal
movement. Nonetheless, there is sufficient evidence within the Kabbalistic and Hasidic literatures to demonstrate that the mystic experience
was not only known but experienced by Jews as a Jewish experience
throughout its history.

For many, if not most, persons who have experienced the mystic
experience, there is a reluctance to speak of it for a number of reasons.
This is no more emphasized in Judaism than in the other monotheistic
traditions, but Judaism does not emphasize other common means of expressing the experience such as poetry in the Sufi tradition and theological discourse in the Christian tradition. The Kabbalah literature tends
toward the practical, including the Hasidic *devekut* (cleaving), which can
include union in and of itself, but the literature focuses on more readily
accessible modes of devotion and devotional practices.

Most important, perhaps, in this relative silence is the understanding
that the supreme, the most holy, of spiritual potentiality is in essence ineffable.

This ineffable quality is in itself an aspect of the holiness of the experience and, therefore, must be honored. It is said of the Great Maggid,

> Once the Rabbi admonished someone because he was dis-
> cussing Kaballah in public. " . . . but you discuss everything that
> is written in '*Ez Hayyim* literally, and thus you transform the
> spiritual into the corporeal; but the sublime, the spiritual world
> is [indeed] ineffable." (Idel, *Hasidism* 235)

CHRISTIANITY

Christianity is far less homogeneous than either Judaism or Islam, not that the latter two general traditions do not encompass a variety of religious approaches. Although there are far more than three major branches of Christianity, the discussion will be limited to the European traditions: Catholicism, Orthodoxy, and Protestantism, with little discussion of the latter.

Protestantism, as a whole, focuses more on direct experience of the sacred text as a book than on personal religious experience tangentially related to the book. Of course, given the wide variety of traditions within Protestantism, there are a number of variants that have run counter to this general tendency. The Quakers, for example, focus on a personal relationship and understanding of deity but have not left a major literature on these experiences and interpretations thereof. Pentecostalism focuses on ecstatic religious experiences with an emphasis on possession by the Holy Spirit. Undoubtedly, some, if not many, Pentecostals do have the mystic experience, but it is difficult to recognize it with certainty given their traditional rhetoric. Hence, in this section, the discussion will focus on two major Christian traditions—the Roman Catholic and Eastern Orthodox—which have extensive literature on mysticism but radically differ in their respective Churchs' attitudes toward it.

CATHOLICISM

There is a voluminous literature describing aspects of the mystic experience in the Roman Catholic Church. This discussion will be limited to a half-dozen of the major known authors. (The first mentioned, Psuedo-Dionysius, is as important to the Eastern Orthodox tradition as it is to Roman Catholicism as he lived before the schism between the two.)

Light

Among the earliest, if not the earliest, explicit Christian reference to the mystic experience is in the text of an unknown person called Pseudo-Dionysius who probably lived in the early sixth century. Chapter 1 of *The Mystical Theology* begins with a poem:

> in the brilliant darkness of a hidden silence.
> Amid the deepest shadow
>   they pour overwhelming light
>   on what is most manifest.
> Amid the wholly unsensed and unseen
>   they completely fill our sightless minds
>   with treasures beyond all beauty.
>   (Dupré and Wiseman 83)

Meister Eckhart (1260–c. 1329), whose writings have deservedly become particularly popular for modern comparative studies of mysticism, speaks in a sermon on light:

> Comes then the soul into the unmixed light of God. It is transported so far from creaturehood into nothingness that, of its own powers, it can never return to its agents or its former creaturehood. (Eckhart, modified from the Blakney trans. 159: "unmixed" is the literal rather than Blakney's translation)

The Flemish mystic, Jan van Ruusbroec (1293–1381), also writes of light as the entry to the mystic experience:

> The measureless illumination of God, which together with his incomprehensible resplendence, is a cause of all gifts and virtues is the same incomprehensible light which transforms and pervades our spirit's inclination toward blissful enjoyment. It does this in a way which is devoid of all particular form, since it occurs in incomprehensible light. . . . This call is an overflow of essential resplendence . . . enveloping us in fathomless love, makes us lose ourselves and flow forth into the wild darkness of the God-

head. Thus united . . . we are able to meet God with God and endlessly possess our eternal blessedness with him and in him. (Dupré and Wiseman 183)

John of the Cross (1542–91) in stanza number 4 of "Stanzas of the Soul," the core of *Dark Night*, writes of light:

> This light guided me
> More surely than the light of noonday
> To the place where he (well I know who!) was awaiting me—
> A place where none appeared. (34)

In Jacob Boehme's (an early Lutheran, but analysts of mysticism find his writings closer to the Catholic mysticism of his time) *Six Theosophic Points*, written in 1620, we similarly find the following:

> . . . and the eternal Light cannot be laid hold of by anything, unless that thing fall into death, and give its essence voluntarily to the fire of Nature, and pass with its essential will out of itself into the Light; and abandon itself wholly to the Light; and desire to will or to do nothing, but commit its will to the Light, that the Light may be its will. (57)

In these excerpts, chronologically arranged, and there are many more in the extant literature, what is written is far closer to the authors' experience than to normative theology. As written, three could be from any tradition, and for the other two, if the word "God" is changed to the "Ultimate," they similarly could describe the experiences of virtually anyone who has experienced the "light" as the entry point to self-loss and bliss.

Unknowing, Self-loss, and Union
Meister Eckhart, speaks in a number of different ways on self-loss in his sermons,

> If you could only become unconscious of everything all at once and ignore your own life. . . . This is the way a man should diminish his senses and introvert his faculties until he achieves forgetfulness of things and self. (Blakney trans. 99)

If you are to know God divinely, your own knowledge must become as pure ignorance, in which you forget yourself and every other creature. (Blakney trans. 119)

Further, I say that if the soul is to know God, it must forget itself and lose [consciousness of] itself, for as long as it is self-aware and self-conscious, it will not see or be conscious of God. (Blakney trans. 131)

Chapter 1 of *The Mystical Theology* by Pseudo-Dionysius, with which we began this discussion of Christianity, ends with the following:

. . . and he plunges into the truly mysterious darkness of unknowing. Here, renouncing all that the mind may conceive, wrapped entirely in the intangible and invisible, he belongs completely to him who is beyond everything. Here, being neither oneself nor someone else, one is supremely united by a completely unknowing activity of all knowledge, and knows beyond the mind by knowing nothing. (Dupré and Wiseman 84)

Theresa of Avila (1515–82), the well-known Spanish mystic, writes in *The Interior Castle*:

There is no need here to suspend the mind since all the faculties are asleep in this state—and truly asleep—to the things of the world and to ourselves. . . . In sum, it is like one who in every respect has died to the world so as to live more completely in God. The death is a delightful one. . . . For during the time of this union, it neither sees, nor hears, nor understands, because the union is always short and seems to the soul even much shorter than it probably is. (Dupré and Wiseman 279–80)

With regard to unity, many of the Christian mystics are quite explicit. Eckhart said in a sermon, speaking of the experience, "God and I: we are one" (Blakley trans. 182).

Nothingness
In one of his sermons, Meister Eckhart speaks of God as Zhuang Zhou does of the Dao. Where the latter uses the term, "uncarved block," Eckhart

speaks of God's "undifferentiated essence" (Blakney trans. 98). And, as in early Daoist thought arising from the mystic experience, that which is undifferentiated can be understood equally as all or nothing. Hence, in the passage from Eckhart on undifferentiated light is also the concept of nothingness. Eckhart is speaking of the soul "as transported into nothingness," but by implication, God is then a Nothingness, which is how the Church understood these words, as we shall see. Eckhart returns to this topic in another sermon from a somewhat different perspective:

> . . . there is only unity in the Godhead and there is nothing to talk about. God acts. The Godhead does not. . . . The difference between God and the Godhead is the difference between action and nonaction. . . . [In the Godhead,] even God passes away. (Blakney trans. 226)

Eckhart was not alone in perceiving God as nothingness, as well as equating nothingness with unity. Jan van Ruusbroec writes,

> . . . a person meets God without intermediary, and an ample light shining from out of God's Unity, reveals to him darkness, bareness, and nothingness . . . in the nothingness, all his activity fails him, for he is overcome by the activity of God's fathomless love, while in the inclination of his spirit towards blissful enjoyment he overcomes God and becomes one spirit with him. . . . In the inmost part of his being, in both soul and body, he neither knows or feels anything except a unique resplendence accompanied by a felt sense of well-being and a penetrating savor. (Dupré and Wiseman 183)

Certitude

One of the characteristics of the mystic experience is certainty, lack of doubt. This aspect of the experience is stressed, indeed, perfectly stated, by Theresa,

> God so places Himself in the interior of that soul that when it returns to itself it can in no way doubt that it was in God and God was in it. This truth remains with it so firmly that even though years go by without God's granting that favor again, the soul can neither forget nor doubt that it was in God and God was in it. . . . And I would say that whoever does not receive this

certitude does not experience union of the whole soul with
God. . . . (Dupré and Wiseman 280)

Speaking for myself, over thirty years after the experience, and as found in
the self-reports of decades-old experiences in chapter 2, this certitude never
lessens.

The Church's Reaction

With the development of a fully institutional, hierarchical Roman Catholic
Church by the medieval period, virtually all of the mystics whose writings
have come down to us from that time were monks and nuns, most cloistered.
The most important twentieth-century Catholic mystic, at least for the English language, is probably Thomas Merton, a Trappist monk. Although the
mystic experience is hardly limited among Catholics to those leading the
contemplative life under vows, it is predominantly these that the Church is
comfortable with and publicizes. There are at least two reasons that the
church has not promoted the mystic experience for laypersons.

From the theoretical standpoint, full union between human and God
is not theologically admissible; Creator and created can never be one and
the same. This is a denial of the essential aspect, within the Christian understanding, of the mystic experience. This understanding is patently clear
in the writings of one of the most influential Catholic philosophers of the
twentieth century, Étienne Gilson. On the topic of *unitus spiritus*, he writes:

> For the Christian God is Being—*Ego sum qui sum*—and this cre-
> ative being is radically other than the being of His creatures. . . .
> Thus we are already assured of two closely connected points: the
> soul does not become the substance of God, neither does it lose
> its own being in ecstasy. (120, 123)

Hence, Gilson denies what the Catholic mystics quoted above literally say,
and further denies that a Christian can have the mystic experience and remain a Christian. Of course, Gilson also denies that such an experience is
actually possible; therefore, for him, it is not a threat to Christianity.

The second reason is more practical. The Roman Catholic Church
understands itself to be the intermediary between God and human, and the
sole intermediary at that. The mystic experience, for theists, means a direct
communion between God and human without any intermediary. Thus, the
Church, as it defines itself, loses its essential importance if the validity of the
mystic experience is accepted.

Meister Eckhart is not only the clearest Catholic expositor of a direct unmediated union, he preached it in the vernacular, German, to ordinary people, not limiting his sermons to other monks and nuns learned in Latin and the Church Fathers. His works long disappeared until resurrected with a secular interest in mysticism over a half century ago and has only more recently been accepted in Catholic publications, for Meister Eckhart was charged with heresy and, had he not died before his trial, would probably have been convicted.

The translations of Eckhart quoted above were published in a secular press; three-quarters of the text are translations from his sermons in German. In a more recent translation published by a Catholic press quoted below, but slightly more than 10 percent of the translated material are from the sermons. The bulk of this text consists of translations from Eckhart's writings in Latin. And this is the crux of Eckhart's heresy. He preached in a language ordinary people could understand that they could, indeed, some undoubtedly already had, directly experience God. There was nothing that the Church itself could do to cause the experience; only God could. Needless to say, the Church was not happy with him. In the bull "In agro dominico" (1329) we find:

> We are indeed sad to report that in these days someone by the name of Eckhart from Germany, a doctor of sacred theology (as is said) and a professor of the order of preachers, wished to know more than he should, and not in accordance with sobriety and the measure of faith, because he turned his ear from the truth and followed fables. The man was led astray by the Father of Lies who often turns himself into an angel of light. . . . He [Eckhart] presented many things as dogma that were designed to cloud the true faith in the hearts of many, things which he put forth especially before the uneducated crowd in his sermons and that he also admitted into his writings. (Colledge and McGinn trans. 77)

Note that the bull considers the ecstatic experience of light, so common in the mystic experience, in and of itself to be the work of the Devil. Aside from Eckhart's preaching the experience to the masses, a list of heretical views in his sermons and writings is enumerated. Perhaps the most interesting is the charge against Eckhart for holding to what is a common means of understanding the mystic experience in East and South Asia, as well as in Judaism, that the experience is a null-experience. From the above bull, we find, "The twenty-sixth article. All creatures are one pure nothing. I do not say that they are a little something or anything, but that they are pure nothing" (Colledge and McGinn trans. 80).

Eckhart defended himself to an earlier set of charges in 1326. His defense on the above point is most telling of his approach:

> As for the fifteenth, when it says: "All creatures are pure noth-ing," it must be said that this is pure, devout and useful truth, leading to the formation of character, contempt of the world, love of God, and love of him alone. To believe the opposite of this is the error of inexperience. . . . (Blakney trans. 272)

Eckhart not only reaffirms the truth of nothingness, but posits that if one does not understand it, it simply means that the denier has not had the mystic experience.

Orthodoxy

The stance of the Eastern Orthodox Church is diametrically opposed to that of the Roman Catholic Church on a number of issues, one being the attitude toward the mystic experience. Rather than keeping mystics on the fringes and sequestered as in Catholicism, Orthodoxy considers the experience central to the Church's understanding:

> Far from being mutually opposed, theology and mysticism sup-port and complete each other. One is impossible without the other. . . . There is, therefore, no Christian mysticism without theology; but, above all, there is no theology without mysticism. It is not by chance that the tradition of the Eastern Church has reserved the name of 'theologian' peculiarly for three sacred writ-ers . . . and the third St. Symeon, called the 'New Theologian', the singer of union with God. (Lossky 8–9)

It is on Saint Symeon that this discussion will focus, first, because of the avail-ability of selected translations, and, second, because of his focus on union.

Light

> Again the light illumines me, again it is seen clearly, again it opens the heavens, again it destroys the night, again it makes all things

disappear. Once more it alone is seen, once more it makes me leave the visible realities and likewise, Oh marvel! removes me from the sensible. (Symeon in Krivocheine 228)

Symeon twice explicitly describes his mystic experiences. Both are similar and are identical with many of the self-reports found in the first two chapters of this book. The following is his description of his second experience while a novice in his monastic order:

Suddenly also, falling prostrate on the ground, I saw, and behold! a great light shone intelligibly upon me, attracting my entire mind and soul. I was struck with amazement at the unexpected wonder; I was as in a trance. Nor is this all: I forgot where I was and who I was. I was only content to cry, "*Kyrie eleison,*" so that when I came to my senses, I was surprised to find myself repeating it. . . . That is not all: suddenly an immense joy, a feeling of the spirit, a sweetness surpassing the savor of any visible thing spread over my soul in an indescribable fashion, granting me a liberty and a forgetfulness of all the thoughts of this life, including the manner of my leaving this present world. . . . Indeed, all of the feelings of my spirit as well as my soul were attached to the ineffable bliss of this light, of this light alone. (Krivocheine 217–18)

For Symeon, the mystic experience as a whole is summed up in "light," not, of course, as a metaphor, but as actual experience. For, after all, the light precedes the nothingness (see the following section), after which there is no memory until one returns to normal consciousness. Hence, the light is God Himself: "God is light, a light infinite and incomprehensible. Everything to do with God is light. . . . Accordingly, all that comes from God is light and is imparted to us as arising from the light" (Krivocheine 223). It is in the light that bliss begins, and it is with the light that Symeon remembers bliss: "Light . . . accessible to those in whom it rises, becoming for them ineffable joy, a peace that surpasses all understanding[,] voluptuousness, pleasure, exhilaration—satiation without satiety" (Krivocheine 222).

Union

Then He mingles with the soul but does not blend with it. The One who is pure essence is entirely united with the essence of the soul. . . . How, I cannot tell. The two become one. The soul is united with its Creator and the Creator is in the soul, totally with the soul alone. (Krivocheine 195)

Thus Symeon is explicit with regard to union yet is able to delicately skirt over the concern with identity, which would be heretical within Christianity: "How strange a marvel: my flesh, that is, the essence of my soul, indeed, of my body, partakes of the divine glory. It shines with a divine radiance" (Krivocheine 195).

But ultimately words fail, for this union, this bliss, the understandings that arise from the experience are, after all, ineffable: "I find no words. My mind sees what is being accomplished but cannot explain it. It contemplates; it wants to speak yet finds no word. What it sees is invisible, entirely devoid of form, simple, wholly incomposite, infinite in greatness" (Krivocheine 195). And it is with this very articulateness of "no word" that Symeon so effectively communicates, as did Tao Qian in poem number five of "Twenty Poems after Drinking Wine" (see preceding chapter), the depth of his experience.

Symeon takes the importance of the experience a step beyond the Catholic mystics, for, similar to modern Pentecostalism with regard to possession by the Holy Spirit, he places union as an essential necessity to being a Christian: "But those who have not entered into the knowledge and contemplation of such beauty . . . and have perfect communion with it—tell me, how can they in any way be called Christians? In the true sense they can not" (Krivocheine 164).

On the other hand, even in his own day there were many in the Church who doubted the reality of Symeon's experiences: "They do not believe that in our generation there can be someone who is moved and influenced by the divine Spirit, who perceptibly sees and apprehends Him" (Krivocheine 167).

But without the experience, without experiencing the presence of and merging with God, then one is ignorant of God. Knowledge cannot come from logical cogitation; we can but know what we actually experience:

What is sealed and closed, invisible and unknowable to all men becomes disclosed, visible and knowable to us only through the Holy Spirit. How can those who have never experienced the presence of the Holy Spirit, His radiance and illumination, the visitation (He makes) in them, even possibly know, comprehend or understand even one iota of it? (Krivocheine 173)

Nothingness

As Meister Eckhart, Symeon is not hesitant to call God a "nothing", this being an understanding arising from the mystic experience itself: "He is transcendent and surpasses the understanding of very mind, since He is nothing" (Krivocheine 186: ignoring Krivocheine's addition of "that men can say of him").

> Attend to the mystery of God ineffable: mysteries unutterable, strange, and altogether unheard of. God truly is, He really is . . . but he is nothing, absolutely nothing of all the realities we know, nor of the things which angels know. And in this sense I say: God is nothing, nothing [at] all. (Krivocheine 190: ignoring Krovocheine's addition of "created things")

The Church's Reaction

Perhaps the most telling difference between the Roman Catholic Church and the Eastern Orthodox Church is that Symeon was not charged with heresy for the above statement, whereas Eckhart was. In contrast, Symeon was considered a saint by the Orthodox Church, while Eckhart was forgotten by the Roman Church, until non-Catholics celebrated his understanding in the twentieth century.

There are a number of reasons for this difference. For one, the Eastern Church is not as rigidly hierarchical as the Roman Church; it allows for both regional and individual differences. And, in part, the latter is due to the Eastern Church placing primacy of experience over intellectual understanding. Putting precedence on personal experience means accepting that there will always be individual variations. It is the experience of the Divine presence that makes the Christian, not an avowal of an unexperienced truth. The Divine Light experienced by Symeon, who articulated his experiences, became a profound truth for the Eastern Church

Again differing from Catholicism, Orthodoxy not only accepts the experiences of those who are not cloistered, but celebrates the understandings based on experiences of laypersons: "Eastern hagiography, which is extremely rich, shows beside the holy monks many examples of spiritual perfection acquired by simple laymen and married people living in the world" (Lossky 19).

Also, as in the Sufi tradition, the Eastern Church understands that the experience of the Divine is a personal relationship best kept secret.

The type of autobiographical statements found in the writings of Symeon are rare in the Eastern Church, which is one of the reasons why Symeon is so important to the Church: "The way of mystical union is nearly always a secret between God and the soul concerned, which is never confided to others unless, it may be, to a confessor or to a few disciples" (Lossky 20).

Thus the Eastern Church encourages spiritual practices for all, not just contemplative monks and nuns. To that end, the Church has promoted simple spiritual exercises, such as constant repetition of the "Jesus Prayer" (see Gillet), so that all may become more open to the union experience. Yet the Church also recognizes that no practice mandates experiencing the Divine Light: "All the conditions necessary for attaining this final end are given to Christians in the Church. But union with God is not the result of an organic or unconscious process: it is accomplished in persons by the co-operation of the Holy Spirit and our freedom" (Lossky 216).

ISLAM

. . . . .
I saw the sun, moon, stars and all the lights

. . . . .
Everything came toward me—
Nothing remained that did not—

. . . . .
Sun and moon were veiled
  The stars fell
    The lights died out
      All save he enveloped in darkness
My eye did not see
  My ear did not hear
    My perception failed
Everything spoke saying
  Allahu Akbar!

. . . . .
I fell into the darkness
  And beheld myself
> (from the *Book of Mystical Standings* by Niffari [d. 965]
> in Sells, "Bewildered Tongue" 111–12)

My [ecstatic] existence (*wujūd*) is
  absence from existing,
Through what I was shown
  and witnessed.

(Sufi recitation in Sells, *Early* 113–14)

Within the first few centuries of the establishment of Islam, a mystical strain, known by the term "Sufi" had become entrenched. In this tradition, the essential aspects of the mystic experience are clearly enumerated, as expressed earlier. Already in the Qur'an there is a term for deity that is the essence of the mystic experience, the "real," that allowed for direct descriptions of the experience. And a practice of giving precedence to individualistic private understandings of mystic experiences lessened the concern for theological correctness. Hence, Islamic expressions and expositions of this experience, particularly the aspect of self-loss, tend to be far closer to a description of actual experience than many of those in Judaism and Christianity. Islam is the one tradition of the Religions of the Book that evidences little if any discomfort with total union, because it fully understands this union within the context of complete loss of self.

This discourse on the mystic experience as understood within Islam will focus on the categories of light; reality; self-loss, including bliss and union; and silence or secrecy. Save for a direct discussion with a Sufi adept in Konya, this discourse is entirely based on the superb scholarship of Michael Sells, especially his focus on the communication of the mystic experience, as well as his translations of the relevant texts, although the interpretations are mine.

LIGHT

Within the Qur'an, the *Sura of Light* (24:35) is the basic sacred text for this aspect of the mystic experience:

> God is the light of the heavens and earth.
>   The light like the light of a lamp in a niche
> The lamp enclosed in a cover of glass
> The glass like a glistening star
> Kindled from the oil of a blessed tree
> An olive not from the East nor the West

Its light glows forth nearly without the touch of fire
Light on light God guides to his light whomever he will
Allah strikes symbols for humankind
Allah in all things is most knowing.

(Sells, *Early* 91–92)

The image is put in terms of a symbol, but a symbol hardly requires such detail, with an emphasis on a light without heat like no other, brilliant and colorless. Hence, the *sura* could and has been interpreted as the light experienced in moving toward, in Islamic mystical terms, the "Real": "Light on light God guides to his light whomever he will." Mohammad Sahl ibn at-Tustar' (d. 986) is quoted by his follower Muhammad ibn Sālim commenting on this verse: ". . . behind the names and the attributes are attributes that cannot be penetrated by understanding because the real is a raging fire. There is no way there. There is no choice but to plunge into it" (Sells, *Early* 95).

AL-HAQQ, "THE REAL"

As the mystic experience defines for those who have the experience true reality, besides which all else is false, in Islamic mysticism, the simple term, "the real," becomes synonymous with the absolute, the ultimate, Allah. "The Qur'an placed the term in apposition to Allah, and thus it became commonly identified with the deity" (Sells, *Mystical* 64). For the Sufi, I would assume, the real was more than another name for Allah, it literally designates the emotional/intellectual response to actual experience. The real expresses precisely all that can be assuredly said of *fanā'*, loss of self, and *baqā'*, upon returning.

FANĀ', THE "PASSING AWAY" OF THE SELF

In Islam, there is a greater willingness to give precedence to experience over theology. Abū l-Qāsim al-Junayd (d. 910) writes of critics, "How then can they describe or find what they have not undertaken, what they have not borne upon themselves, what they have not approached, that of which they have no knowledge." This in regard to the loss of self: "So we said that the real annihilates anything to which it appears, and when it subjugates, it is first in subjugating and most real in overcoming and overpowering." This annihilation is bliss in and of itself: "They find bliss hidden in it, through enjoyment of existence in the mode of nonexistence, insofar as the real has taken exclusive possession and complete subjugation." (All the above from Sells, *Early* 261–62.)

This bliss is termed *wajd* (ecstasy). 'Abd al-Karīm ibn Hawāzin al-Qushayrī (d. 1074) writes, "As for ecstatic existentiality (*wujūd*), it occurs after one rises beyond *wajd*. There is no existential ecstatic experience (*wujūd*) of the real except after the extinction of the mortal." Qushayrī quotes the Sufi recitation quoted above at the beginning of the section on Islam. The extinction is total. Qushayrī writes, "When effacement comes to dominate a person, however, he has no knowledge, no reason, no understanding, and no sense." And in this extinction is ultimate union. According to Qushayrī,

> But if he is snatched from all regard of creation, uprooted from his own self, utterly removed from perceiving any 'other' through the sovereign power of reality when it appears and seized him, that is union of union (*jam' al-jam*). . . . Union of union is the utter perishing and passing away of all perception of any other-than-God, Most Glorious and Sublime, through the onslaughts of reality. (Sells, *Early* 113–18)

As in other traditions, including other monotheistic traditions exemplified in Eckhart, this extinction leads to speaking of the ultimate as an utter negative, a nothingness. Rumi (d. 1273) wrote, "I will become nothing, for nonexistence calls to me in deafening tune: 'Unto Him we shall return'" (Qur'an 2:156, quoted by Chittick 79).

BAQĀ', THE "REMAINING" OR "RETURN" OF CONSCIOUSNESS

This extinction, of course, is but temporary, and this coming back into normal existence—"waking consciousness" (*sahw*)—is called "second separation" (*al-farq ath-thanī*). (The first separation is the realization of the possibility of union through the experience of others.) But on the "second separation" there is no memory of union, for the person, as Qushayrī puts it,

> has no knowledge of self or creatures, no perception, no information, so that even if self and creatures exist, he is utterly unaware of

them, not perceiving them in any way. . . . When the servant passes away from the attribute through which his memory operates, then he rises from that through passing away from the vision of his own passing away. . . . Then there is a person's passing away from witnessing his own passing away through his perishing in the ecstatic existentiality (*wujūd*) of the real. (Sells, *Early* . . . 121)

SIRR, "SECRECY," "MYSTERY"

Not long ago, I had the opportunity to speak to Sufi adepts in their heartland, the city of Konya in Turkey. I learned that adepts can, if Allah wills, achieve the mystic experience within their twirling dance-meditations. This is possible, I assume, because the long training leads to routinized motions that require no conscious control. The twirling dances, which I was able to observe, clearly lead to trance states, which while initiated by the music, go on in and of themselves once established.

More important, I was told that whatever one experiences through the ritualized meditations is not imparted to others. It is a private experience, an experience with and in the "real," which excludes all other experiences. The discussion that I had was not a normal one. First, I had to speak through an interpreter, who was a modern-educated Muslim, and instruct the interpreter to translate what I said and the responses absolutely literally. Hence, the communication took place through an intermediary who did not understand what we were talking about, which allowed us privacy. Second, the discussion involved more silence than words. We both could look into each other eyes and but communicate that each knew precisely the subject matter of the other. And nothing further in that regard needed to be said. The question was answered.

The tendency in the Sufi tradition is to express one's understanding through love poetry, as also occurred in India, or with allusions to drunkenness, as was the case in China. It is the love metaphor that explains in part the importance of secrecy, for one does not betray through exposure the relationship between lover and beloved (Sells, "Bewildered Tongue" 91). But secrecy has other advantages. On the one hand, it accepts the nature of the ineffable. Hence, it is best not to talk about what cannot be talked about. On the other hand, it avoids the possibility of threatening the theological sensibilities of those who have not had the experience. The Sufi tradition is far from the only tradition in which discretion concerning one's mystical experience is preferred, if not mandated.

SYNTHESIS

The founders of the Sufi traditions of contemporary central Turkey originally came from central Asia to the east, where Buddhism has long been established. It is hardly surprising that many Buddhist spiritual customs were integrated, such as the use of prayer beads (which maintain the Buddhist form). But Islam also took over large parts of South Asia, and there arose in India Sufi writings that incorporated the flavor of Hindu mysticism without any actual change in the Sufi understanding. An example of this development will be found in the writings of Shaikh Sharaf ud-dīn Yahyā of Manīr, whose writings would date to the end of the fourteenth or the beginning of the fifteenth centuries:

> . . . the stage of complete absorption, i.e., losing the very consciousness of being absorbed and of seeking after God—for such a consciousness still implies separation. Here, the soul merges itself and the universe into the Divine Light, and loses the consciousness of merging as well. . . . Here there is neither formulae nor ceremonies, neither being nor nonbeing, neither description nor illusion, neither heaven nor earth. It is this stage alone that reveals the mystery. . . . Absolute unity without duality is realized here. (de Bary 423)

In summary, in Islam, differing from Christianity, there is no fear of the experience of union denying a distinction between God and human:

> I am you,
> you,
>   my being,
>   end of my desire.
>   (from the *Dīwān* attributed to al-Hallaj, Sells, *Early* 302)

MODERN "SECULAR" MYSTICISM

In Western Europe, perhaps due to the relative aridity of Roman Catholicism and mainstream Protestantism with regard to religious experience, particularly for laypersons, a host of alternative movements developed among small numbers of people. Rosicrucians, Freemasons,

Swedenborgians are among the earlier spiritual explorers followed by Transcendentalists, Theosophists, Spiritualists, and others. The latter movements included openness to a variety of non-Western religious traditions, usually understood in a highly selective manner. The so-called New World, specifically the United States, which in its inception attempted to throw off many of the Old World's shackles, including religious orthodoxy, was particularly rich in these developments. In a sense, the World Parliament of Religions held in Chicago at the end of the nineteenth century marked a culmination of these tendencies. It brought a general awareness of East and South Asian religions to a much broader population, and it left behind religious leaders from Asia to found distinctively Western versions of these traditions.

Following World War II, a new internationalism was found in the United States, and the end of colonialism in Europe led to new attitudes toward former colonies. Aldous Huxley's *The Perennial Philosophy* and other books brought the idea of a generalized worldwide mysticism to the attention of the reading public. Zen Buddhism, particularly as popularized by D. T. Suzuki and Alan Watts, became known to virtually all American intellectuals, and Hinduism, especially Vedanta, and Buddhism became of increasing interest to the British. Two decades later, due to the emigration of the monks on one side of a schism resulting from political turmoil in their homeland, Tibetan Buddhism replaced Zen Buddhism as the Western Buddhism of choice. Another two decades saw a Western Daoism, one that would be unrecognizable in China, begin to become popular.

Many of the more recent developments can be assumed under the rubrics of "Transpersonal Psychology," discussed in an earlier chapter, and "New Age religion." Interconnected, based on earlier developments, both began in the 1960s and slowly flourished. Their histories and approaches are too complex to briefly summarize, but readers are recommended to an anthology, with many excellent essays, and a study with a historical perspective: respectively, *Perspectives on the New Age*, edited by James R. Lewis and Gordon Melton; and *New Age Religion and Western Culture*, by Wouter J. Hanegraaff.

In these developments, the mystic experience per se is of minor importance. For the purpose of this discussion, two strands that do focus on the experience will be analyzed: the "Cosmic Consciousness" of Richard Bucke and the cosmic "Absolute Consciousness" of Stanislav Grof, representing a precursor to the New Age and a mainstay of transpersonal psychology, respectively.

Cosmic Consciousness

In the 1970s, a sufficient number of students approached me at the universities where I taught to teach them to achieve "cosmic consciousness" that I came to cringe whenever I heard the term. The term and concept come from a book that has remarkably been in print for a full century, and, in many respects, is the forerunner of what might be called, "science fiction mysticism," as found, for example, in the writings of Arthur C. Clarke, such as the novel *Childhood's End,* and his screenplay for the film *2001.*

Richard Maurice Bucke wrote *Cosmic Consciousness: A Study in the Evolution of the Human Mind* a year before his accidental death in 1901. He was born in Canada in 1837 and already had lived a diverse life before entering medical school and subsequently becoming a well-known psychiatrist, having been president of both British and American psychiatric associations and a professor of psychiatry. As well, he was good friends with a number of eminent persons of his day, including Walt Whitman.

At the age of thirty-six, while in England, he had an experience that had a profound influence on his understanding, an experience that was the basis of his book (he writes of himself in the third person):

> All at once, without warning of any kind, he found himself wrapped around as it were by a flame colored cloud. For an instant he thought of fire, some sudden conflagration in the great city, the next he knew that the light was within himself. Directly afterwards came upon him a sense of exaltation, of immense joyousness, accompanied or immediately followed by an intellectual illumination quite impossible to describe. . . . The illumination itself continued not more than a few moments, but the effects proved ineffaceable; it was impossible for him ever to forget what he at that time saw and knew, neither did he, or could he, ever doubt the truth of what was then presented to his mind. (8)

Bucke understood that he had experienced "Brahmic Splendor" and felt "Brahmic Bliss," both probably understood from transcendentalist writings; further:

> He saw and knew that the Cosmos is not dead matter but a living Presence, that the soul of man is immortal, that the universe is so built and ordered that without any peradventure all things work

together for the good of each and all, that the foundation principle of the world is what we call love and that the happiness of every one is in the long run absolutely certain. (8)

Bucke lived in an age when biological evolution was a new and fascinating theme. He came to understand that having the experience initiated one into a new phase of mammalian evolution, based on a trinitarian model of consciousness. The first evolutionary phase is Simple Consciousness, found in non-human mammals. The second phase is Self Consciousness, found in the superior human race(s?)—excluded are "many members of low races, such as the Bushmen of South Africa and native Australians" (39). The third phase is Cosmic Consciousness, found, in effect, in a new race of *übermensch*, consisting of all those who have had the mystic experience: "Cosmic Consciousness, then, is a higher form of consciousness than that possessed by ordinary man" (1):

> Cosmic Consciousness is a third form which is as far above Self Consciousness as is that above Simple Consciousness. . . . The prime characteristic of cosmic consciousness is, as its name implies, a consciousness of the cosmos, that is, of the life and order of the universe . . . Along with the consciousness of the cosmos there occurs an intellectual enlightenment or illumination which alone would place the individual on a new plane of existence—would make him almost a member of a new species. . . . With these come, what may be called, a sense of immortality, a consciousness of eternal life, not a conviction that he shall have this, but the consciousness that he has it already. (2)

Statistics are presented to argue that the experience was becoming more frequent among Caucasians who are evolving into a new race based on cosmic consciousness. This is now available to all who meet the right conditions, including that of heredity. Bucke wrote his book to assist others in reaching his superior state of consciousness. When humans reach this new plane of existence,

> In contact with the flux of cosmic consciousness all religions known and named today will be melted down. The human soul will be revolutionized. . . . The world peopled by men possessing cosmic consciousness will be as far removed from the world

of today as this is from the world as it was before the advent of self consciousness [i.e., before the rise of humans]. (4)

But this is the certain future, for in his present time, Bucke assumes that the experience he had occurs to but "one in many millions" (43). Bucke was privileged indeed; but he assumes that more and more individuals, with the correct prerequisites, will have the experience:

> Cosmic Consciousness, then, appears in individuals mostly of the male sex, who are otherwise highly developed—men of good intellect, of high moral qualities, of superior physique. It appears at about that time of life when the organism is at its high watermark of efficiency, at the age of thirty to forty years. (55)

Bucke, of course, has described the Victorian notion of a proper gentleman, in all of its androcentric, racist glory.

But at the time Bucke wrote his treatise in 1900, a new literature was beginning that was also futuristic, with such writers as Jules Verne and H. G. Wells. This literature tended also to be evolutionary, positing that future humans would have a "higher," superior consciousness. In some of this literature, the cosmos itself was a spiritual organism with which humans could identify and merge, or the Cosmos itself was an all-encompassing being that was a spiritual teacher. In this sense, Bucke, unwittingly, had a major impact on what developed into the amorphous New Age movement.

Absolute Consciousness

As discussed in chapter 4, Abraham Maslow was one of the pioneering psychotherapists who saw religious experience not ipso facto as a sign of mental illness but as a constituent of a healthy human being. His concept of "peak-experiences" would include, among other religious experiences, the mystic experience. He understood these peak-experiences, all involving individual transcendence, to be the bases of all religions, as well as the healthy, fully functioning person. Maslow is one of the founding influences on the development of transpersonal psychology. Among the leading members of this movement, Stanislav Grof, along with Ken Wilber, has particularly focused, although not exclusively, on the mystic experience.

Grof centers his approach on the type of experience described by a colleague in psychiatry, who had the experience at the age of thirty-seven:

> The beginning of the experience was very sudden and dramatic, I was hit by a cosmic thunderbolt of immense power that instantly shattered and dissolved my everyday reality. I completely lost contact with the surrounding world; it disappeared as if by magic. . . . At that time, my only reality was a mass of swirling energy of immense proportions that seemed to contain all of Existence in an entirely abstract form. It had the brightness of myriads of suns, yet it was not on the same continuum with any light I knew from everyday life . . . I had no categories for what I was witnessing. I could not maintain a sense of separate existence in the face of such a force. My ordinary identity was shattered and dissolved; I became one with the Source. Time lost any meaning whatsoever. (*Cosmic Game* 28)

In discussing coming out of what is undoubtedly the mystic experience, which lasted twenty minutes, the author of the report used words such as "ecstatic" and "bliss."

Grof considers this one mode of experiencing the "supreme principle in the cosmos or ultimate reality": an "encounter with Absolute Consciousness or identification with it." The other mode "is the identification with Cosmic Emptiness and Nothingness described in the mystical literature as the void" (29–30). Grof does note that "people who experienced both the Absolute Consciousness and the Void had the insight that these two states are essentially identical and interchangeable," although he assumes, as I do not, that they are "experientially distinguished from each other." Yet again he recognizes that "Others experienced these two aspects of the Absolute simultaneously, identifying the Cosmic Consciousness and, at the same time, recognizing its essential voidness" (32).

Based on these experiences, these "holotropic states of consciousness," of others—seemingly not from his own—Grof creates a "theology." The material world of ordinary consciousness does not exist in and of itself; rather, "it is a creation of Absolute Consciousness," "a divine play created by Absolute Consciousness and the Cosmic Void":

> Since in our true nature we are identical with the cosmic creative principle, we cannot assuage our cravings by pursuits in the ma-

terial world, no matter what their nature and scope. Nothing
short of the experience of mystical unity with the divine source
will quench our deepest longing. (39–40)

If Grof is serious about the need for persons to have the actual mystic
experience, as in his example above, in order to be fully healthy from the
mental standpoint, then the majority of humans may be doomed to frustration and a life of illness. For, as discussed above, the experience is nonpre-
dictable and does not occur to everyone. Fortunately, later in his text, Grof
speaks of Maslow's peak-experience as what he has in mind. For there are
many types of peak-experiences—Grof provides a number of examples—
which are available to virtually everyone.

7

Conclusions:
The Mystic Experience
and Human Nature

A PHENOMENOLOGICAL ASSESSMENT

My earliest set of memories consists of images surrounding a bout of acute appendicitis and resulting peritonitis at the age of three, which I barely survived. But the earliest vivid memory took place at the age of four, and it is the strange one that I related in chapter 2, the one in which I am leaning against a jeep facing the low-rise apartment building in which my family lived. And I am wondering what I am—not who I am. That is it.

I have always known that to be my most important early memory; even the age I was at the time is part of the memory itself. After the event described at the beginning of chapter 1, it occurred to me that I had had the mystic experience when I was four. With nothing to fall back on at such an young age, my only possible response to the experience was to ponder the nature of existence itself and to preserve the understanding that something ultimately profound had happened to me. Given that children are prone to, indeed seek, ecstatic experiences, I can but speculate whether my childhood experience is common or uncommon. Certainly the experience itself is far from rare; several other examples are also provided in chapter 2.

Yin Zhiping (1169–1251), who succeeded the founder as leader of the Quanzhen sect of Daoism told a disciple, approximately sixty years after the fact, of an experience he had when five years old (Chinese count, probably four by Western count):

137

> Rapt in my thoughts, I sat under a large mulberry tree. Gazing
> above and below I inquired as to [a series of existential ques-
> tions]. As my pondering and observations came to their limits, I
> arrived at non-thinking. . . . Darkly and murkily, while unaware,
> my mind and body were both lost. Some of my relatives eventu-
> ally came looking for me, and called and wakened me (from my
> trance). It was already evening. (Eskildsen 140)

One wonders if after six decades, Yin or the person recording his musings
had not reversed the experience, that the existential questioning followed
rather than preceded the experience. As with others, it is only later in life
that Yin realizes the import of his early experience: "Later . . . I came to
understand the significance of this oblivion of mind."

Given the childhood experiences reported in chapter 2 and Yin's
account, it is quite possible that many young children have had the mystic
experience. For it is only if one again has the experience when one is more
mature, particularly if one is aware of its cultural or religious importance, is
it likely that the nature of the childhood experience will be recognized.

As mentioned previously, I have been teaching a full-year course on
mysticism, limited to thirty students, for a quarter of a century. After several months, when the more astute students realized I did understand the
subject matter and that they could trust me, there were invariably several
students who imparted to me in private their own mystic experiences.
They were always, from my perception, genuine. Now it is the case that
the students, to a degree, were a self-selective group, given the subject
matter of the course. But an average of approximately 10 percent still suggests that the experience occurs at the very least to one in a hundred in
the population as a whole. My conjecture is corroborated by Greeley's
findings from the National Opinion Research Center's survey discussed in
chapter 4. Applying the survey to the population of the United States as
a whole, one out of every five persons has had a unitive or other similar
ecstatic experience, and possibly as many as one out of ten has had the
mystic experience.

On the other hand, the literature on the subject matter, with few exceptions—William James, Bharati, Stace, Forman, and others—suggests that
the experience is either rare or impossible. Those within highly institutionalized religious traditions, such as Catholicism or Buddhism, would prefer
to understand the experience to occur to the occasional saint or equivalent,
but not to an average person. There is also the tendency to insist that only

those within their organizational structure and ideological framework can have such an experience.

Others, who choose to limit their understanding to the product of a highly structured logic, find that an ineffable experience is impossible. The only aspect of such studies that is certain is that the authors themselves have not had the experience, and, therefore, assume no one else can. It would be as if a congenitally blind person insisted that there was no such phenomenon as sight, as he or she had never perceived it. Those who assume they have had such an experience accordingly must either be deluded or lying. Or such thinkers may conclude that all experiences are mediated by culture and a human experience in and of itself is impossible. They seem to ignore the fact that humans are biological entities, and we essentially are all the same in our neurophysiology, save for the major differences between female and male brains. All cultures, for example, have music; it is but tonal, melodic, and rhythmic structure that varies from culture to culture. Yet music is sufficiently similar cross-culturally that we recognize music as music (we may or may not enjoy it) even in cultures we had not previously encountered.

If we correlate the results of the sociological studies with the majority of studies in the philosophy of religion that, in effect, deny the mystic experience, at least as a human rather than a cultural experience, it seems that these philosophers are a select group that differ from the normal population. They seem to be predominantly those who are not prone to paranormal, let alone ecstatic, experiences. This leads to further speculation as to why these particular scholars have chosen to study mysticism of all possible research topics. Are they devoting their careers to prove that no one can have an experience they themselves have not had? None of us can have all the experiences possible to humans, but that does not deny their reality. As a male, I have never experienced pregnancy, childbirth, or breast-feeding, but I cannot imagine trying to prove that other humans have never had such an experience. Nor do I assume that the essential features of these experiences are different in different cultures, although the hermeneutics will differ.

Academic studies of the mystic experience tend to be disadvantaged in two ways. First, there is a tendency to lump all ecstatic experiences together, as, for example, some early transpersonal psychologists and their precursors perceived a simple dichotomy between "normal consciousness" and "alternate state of consciousness." Such a dichotomy may be useful for certain types of analyses, but it does not help in understanding a specific type of ecstatic experience. Others perceive an all-inclusive, generalized mysticism, focusing on various assumed traits, rather than the experiences in and of themselves. Such studies can lead to generalization that have no validity with regard to experiences people actually have. To the contrary, a few scholars have had one particular kind of ecstatic experience and have assumed that to be the only such experience, accordingly basing their analyses of mysticism in general on the single type of experience.

Second, as also previously pointed out, academics and other scholars have been constrained to avoid mentioning their own ecstatic experiences. For some reason, there is a general understanding that a scholar who has had an ecstatic experience is biased in analyzing it, or, even more insidious, a true scholar would live a life of nonstop formal, modern Western logic and, therefore, could not have such an experience. In no other scholarly endeavor are these standards applied. Who would value an art historian who was unfortunately blind from birth, or a musicologist who was congenitally deaf? Yet this is exactly what is expected of a scholar of ecstatic experiences, save for contemporary anthropology, where participant observation has become an acceptable methodology. As Fritz Staal bluntly states at the beginning of his book, "In the study of mysticism a common drawback is lack of experience." Fortunately, in the last decade or so, several scholars have been forthright about their own experiences.

The first academic I am aware of who explicitly admitted to and described his own mystic experience is Bharati, and it is that "coming out" that led me to admit to my own ecstatic experiences—shamanistic, visionary, and unitive, as well as the mystic experience—and base all of my studies on those experiences as well as the experiences of others, particularly those related to me firsthand. One does not have to have had the mystic experience to fruitfully study it, but studies that argue that the experience cannot happen or are misunderstood by those who assume they have had them are an enormous waste of intellect. Certainly the examples provided in chapters 1, 2, 5, and 6, as well as the survey discussed in chapter 4, clearly establish that there is a definable, human experience with multiple common characteristics, centering on the ecstasy of self-loss, I have labeled the "mystic experience" and laid out in outline form in chapter 1.

Of the various scholarly approaches to the mystic experience, few have proven worthwhile. The discipline of philosophy has, in the main, focused on the nature and possibility of the experience, pro and con. Given that the modern discipline is largely based on a rigorous analysis of language, it is of limited usefulness in discussing an ineffable experience. Psychological analyses, with few exceptions, have either looked upon ecstatic states as indicative of psychopathology or the culmination of mental development. Neither opposing valuations fits the mystic experience. Those whom I have met who have had the mystic experience seem to be fully functioning and relatively happy human beings, not mentally ill, yet I find no reason to assume they are necessarily better developed mentally than others (after all, I have graded the papers and examinations of those who were my students). Those aspects of transpersonal psychology that seemingly are basing a new religion on the mystic experience, which is haphazard in its occurrence, are, at best, likely to engender frustration in its adherents more than anything else. Sociology can but point to the commonality of ecstatic experiences and the fact that they tend to be understood as religious by the many who have them, although the factor analysis in Greeley's study does suggest some interesting avenues for further research. Anthropology can explore the understanding of the mystic experience in human cultures, and this study is to a degree an anthropological approach, although I situate myself in the social science version of comparative religion (history of religions), which incorporates ethnology and ethnohistory. Biology, specifically the neurosciences, discounting those works that are actually theological rather than biological, is just beginning to facilitate the understanding of the mystic experience with regard to its appearance in the human organism. Such studies need not be understood as reductionist. Certainly, Austin has not taken that position, since he reflects on his own experiences, nor do I.

Given that the mystic experience is a common human experience, the understandings and significance of the experience will vary from culture to culture. That is, we as humans seek to understand what we experience, and we can only do that based on what we already know. As humans we are enculturated beings. The very nature of being human includes being brought up in a culture that provides us with an interpretive framework for understanding ourselves and our experiences; that is, we do not exist on pure instinct. Thus, it is not enough to recognize the basic, common aspects of the mystic experience. We need to understand how, from different cultural standpoints, we allow the experience to influence our understanding and our lives; that is, how different cultures deal with the experience. In doing so, we are examining the meanings within cultures of the experience, or, to use a new technical term, the ethnohermeneutics of the mystic experience.

COMPARATIVE ETHNOHERMENEUTICS

In chapter 5, we saw how the mystic experience was understood by an individual within a culture in transition whose traditional religious understanding focused on shamanistic experience. As he lived relatively recently, it was possible to gain an understanding of his life and religious activities, to understand how and why he focused on the experience.

The causal factor leading to the transition of John-Paul from shaman to mystic (and shaman again in the last decade of his life following the renewed interest of a few youths in traditional Anishnabe religion) was his loss of social function because of the transformation if not the near disintegration of his society. Anishnabe religion had undergone a number of transitions following contact with European civilization; from a gathering-hunting democratized-shamanistic culture to a fur-trapping, trading culture to semipermanent and permanent, larger settlement patterns and the development of semi-institutionalized shamanism, the Midéwiwin, and, in modern times, to fixed settlements (reserves) where the traditional clan heads and charismatic leaders had been replaced at Euroamerican insistence by elected, politically instead of spiritually based, "chiefs."

By the mid-twentieth century, socioeconomic patterns and resources came from without the community through Christian churches, public schools, and government-supplied monetary payments (welfare, etc.), and the indigenous religion almost disappeared, excepting unchecked, negatively oriented sorcery (Bearwalking) directed inward toward members of the group, making almost impossible the continuation of what little social interaction remained. Rogers (*Round Lake* E7) found that

> the Round Lake Community [northern Ojibwe in Western Ontario] no longer forms a society in the strict meaning of the word. Certain structures necessary for the group to operate as an autonomous unit now exist external to the community within Canadian society. . . . [Furthermore], there is no overall authority structure . . . nor is there now any religious organization of a single homogeneous nature which might unify the group. . . . Economic organization is restricted primarily to the household level.

The disintegration was similar, if not more severe, in the Manitoulin area. John-Paul illustrates the role of the mystic experience within a particular culture at a stage prior to its integration into a culture should such take place. His situation resulted from a series of religio-ecological transformations of Anishnabe culture over the last three centuries in response to contact with European culture and domination by Euroamerican governments, almost ending in the virtual disappearance of a viable culture. Among many examples of the combined effects of social and cultural disintegration in the Manitoulin area at that time was the "suicide epidemic" of youths at Wikwemikong (Ward, Ward and Fox). The transformation of John-Paul from shaman to mystic between approximately 1940 and 1950 is coincident with the then near termination of Anishnabe religion. (For details of the above and following cultural and socioeconomic transitions and transformations, see Paper, *The Spirits* chap. 5.)

In the last few decades, there has been a significant revitalization of traditional Anishnabe religion. Indeed, traditional ceremonies, including those of the Midéwiwin, are now held on Manitoulin Island and other related reserves. At Wikwemikong, traditional Native healers work with Western physicians. John-Paul would have had a very different life in relation to his community had he lived into the late 1980s.

The situation of John Paul has parallels with China in regard to the relationship between functioning ecstatically and the mystic experience. During the time of Zhuang Zhou twenty-four hundred years ago, discussed in earlier chapters, Chinese culture was also undergoing profound change, a change as important and immense as that of twentieth-century China. By his time, many religio-ecological features of the preceding period had disappeared.

The transformation began at least twenty-six hundred years ago, reaching its culmination twenty-two hundred years ago with the unification of China under the centrist policies of the Qin state and a mercantile, metropolitan economy. Prior to this period, Chinese culture was quasi-feudal, primarily divided into two classes: a hereditary aristocracy composed of literate, professional warrior-ritual specialists with a clan orientation living in an advanced, bronze-using culture; and peasants, using stone tools, living a life little changed from the late Neolithic period.

During the transformation, we find "dissemination of iron agricultural implements on a significant scale" and "verified evidence of the use of human, animal and green manure" (Ho 83); soybean culture had become widespread, allowing with millet effective crop rotation and a source of agricultural protein. The economically self-sufficient manorial system was disappearing to be replaced by private ownership of land and state land taxes. This led to a greater differentiation between classes: those who accumulated land, especially the new, rising merchant class, and the peasants who became hired laborers. The merchant class was an effect of the development of specialized trades and regional economic independence. All of these factors, especially the use of cast iron for agricultural implements, led to considerably increased agricultural efficiency, allowing the growth of large metropolitan manufacturing and mercantile centers at the junction of trade routes, in comparison to the much smaller fortress administrative centers of the preceding period.

Other developments at this time had major effects on the traditional aristocracy. Chariot warfare (aristocratic warriors) was replaced by the use of infantry (peasant-soldiers) leading to considerably larger armies. Calvary was adopted from the northern nomadic tribes (Hsü 68–70). By this period too, the shift from hereditary officials to those chosen for their qualifications enhanced the increasing social mobility within the culture. All these changes led to considerable intellectual ferment, and many of the new ideas are promoted or attacked in the *Zhuangzi*, whose original author clearly enjoyed intellectual debate.

With the weakening of the traditional extended noble families, virtually defined by clan myth and ritual, manorial agriculture on which it was superimposed, and the relationship between these families based on allegiance to the king expressed ritually, a profound transformation of religion is to be expected. As early as the beginning of this transition, we find Kongzi (Confucius) concerned about the decline of interest in the traditional elite rites and ritual relationships. It is at the peak of this major transformation of China's cultural ecology that we find in the *Zhuangzi* evidence for another religious transformation, from remnants of an earlier, now virtually unknown, type of elite shamanism to the initial, unintegrated stage of mysticism (to be integrated into the cultural milieux in the following century), with mediumistic experiences among virtually all of the elite and religious specialists continuing unchanged. This transformation was due not only to this aspect of shamanism losing its function in the distant past, seemingly replaced by specialist mediums, but to a number of the aristocrats losing theirs at the time as well.

The author of the early strata of the *Zhuangzi*, from his education, literacy, and concerns, was clearly from an aristocratic background. Yet the few hints of his living conditions indicates a lifestyle only marginally above that of the peasants. Religion of the family is not only ignored, but even opposed in the few passages concerning ritual. The author clearly had no social function; anecdotes about Zhuang Zhou demonstrate a strong disinclination for government service, the sole elite occupation of the time. Unconnected to the basic elite social unit of the extended family, the larger clan, or the state, the socially afunctional author, prone to ecstatic experience, had mystic experience(s), and discussed them with terminology based on remnants of the earlier *xian* shamanism.

That the *xian* was a shaman who had become transformed at the end of the Zhou period has been previously noted by other scholars, for example, Edward Schafer (11): "But the *hsien* [*xian*] had abandoned the helpful social role of the ancient shamans and, like most Taoists [Daoists], looked only for their own salvation. However, they had not forgotten the archaic techniques of soul projection, and they continued to dream of magic flight to paradises in the sea and air."

It is fortuitous to have any indication for an individual of a shift in the nature of a person's orientation toward ecstatic experience. Both John-Paul and Zhuang Zhou are individual cases of such transformations. Yet the seeming similarity of their experiences indicates the potential for generalization. Thiel (203) raised the question of how shamanism developed into classical, philosophical Daoism (not the latter institutional Daoism) as found in the *Zhuangzi*. The life of the shaman John-Paul, from the opposite side of the globe from China and chronologically distant by nearly two and a half millennia, provides a plausible explanation.

The loss of social function, due to religio-ecological transformations, allows the socially afunctional mystic experience to become more important than functional shamanistic trance. The loss of social function also shifts ecstatic religious experience toward individualistic ones. In summary, the mystic experience, which occurs in all cultures and potentially to all humans, becomes valued over other ecstatic religious experiences when a subsistence culture disintegrates, as in the case of John-Paul due to oppression, or socioeconomic developments allow elite individuals the option of an economically unproductive and individualistic existence, as in the case of Zhuang Zhou.

What happened in China must also have taken place, in a general fashion, in South Asia. Given the cyclic notion of time of South Asian civilizations, history writing did not gain the importance that it did in China and the Mediterranean. Nonetheless, the first South Asian texts to refer to the mystic experience do hint at major cultural transformations. The religious teachers in the Upanishads are often from the warrior-ruler caste rather than the priestly caste. The aristocracy had reached the point where those of the ruling class could lead lives that were not only directly nonproductive, but lives without sociopolitical responsibilities. The religious teachers posited a preferred mode of religiosity, a life of leaving society in search of the mystic experience that was counter to the dominant value of fulfilling one's social, economic, and ritual duties. Other changes also noted as having taken place in China by the time of the *Zhuangzi* had also taken place in India, changes of far-reaching consequences for Buddhism, particularly the rise of wealthy merchants who were not of the dominant castes.

In all of these civilizations, we are aware of these early thoughts on the mystic experience because they had been so integrated into the religio-cultural basis that the experience was considered an important part of the respective cultures. For that to happen, major changes in the general cultural understanding of the mystic experience was necessary. No culture, as a whole, is likely to value an experience that is essentially one that leads the experiencer to question existence in and of itself, let alone conventional cultural values and mores.

Hinduism developed as a synthesis of the Vedic sacrificial traditions of the originally cattle-herding, Indo-European-speaking Aryan culture with the poorly understood more earthly (Earth as a female, numinous entity), agricultural orientation of the indigenous South Asian Dravidian-language cultures, combined with the focus on renunciation in search of *moksha* highlighted in the Upanishads. Those oriented toward the mystic experience were encouraged to put off the interest until late in life when one became less productive due to age and had fulfilled family and social expectations. Thus, there was no conflict between duty and denial of duty, of mores and their denial, of living life fully and denying its meaningfulness.

For the vast majority of Hindus, the religious life remains one of fulfilling one's duties and performing daily sacrificial rituals (*pūjā*). But side by side there also exists a vague notion that life (*saṃsāra*) is undesirable, what Agehananda Bharati called the "*moksha* complex" (from personal discussions). This is an opposite notion to those arising out of the Mediterranean world, which sought eternal life. For the term *saṃsāra* assumes that life is eternal and, in essence, consists of suffering; hence, it is ultimately undesirable. Thus, *moksha* is also a spiritual goal but not the focus of the religious life in and of itself, which consists of *pūjā*. Rather than seek *moksha* directly, it is commonly sought vicariously through direct contact by being in the presence (*darshan*) of those assumed to have had the mystic experience. Such a person would be, for example, Satguru Swami Shri Jnanananda Saraswati of Madras, whose self-description of her experience is provided in chapter 2. Thus, in Hinduism, the mystic experience is viewed as the ultimate goal, but, for the vast majority, not a goal around which one organizes one's life. Given the notion of life that understands continuation through transmigration, for most there is no need to rush to remove oneself from it.

At the end of the nineteenth century, there slowly developed a new Hinduism, an English-language Hinduism designed for Western consumption. This was a Hinduism that understood *moksha* not to be the end of life as *saṃsāra* but as eternal life in the Christian sense. Different from the general understanding in India, in these Western oriented modes of religious practice derived from Hinduism, *moksha* could be attained, not through the traditional long-term study of Sanskrit and texts in Sanskrit combined with many years of intense, daily yoga practice, but through repetition of a brief *mantra* (Transcendental Meditation); by joyously, repeatedly singing a song in praise of Krishna (Krishna Consciousness); or by other truncated techniques, often requiring the contribution of large sums of money. While any form of discipline, no matter how limited, can have beneficial effects, one can but wonder if such practices have any relevance with regard to the mystic experience. A marvelous spoof of parallel developments in India itself can be found in G. V. Desani's comic novel, *All About H. Hatter*. But these developments exist because of a real hunger in the West for spiritual experience, as those of whom Bharati (*Ochre Robe* 22) writes, "the hundreds of poor forlorn American youths whom I have seen at Indian railway stations or in the Khatmandu bazaar looking wistfully at U.S. travel posters, empty as yet of India's recondite wisdom but full of amoebic dysentery."

Buddhism is unique among the world's religions with regard to the mystic experience. For theoretically in Buddhism, *nirvāna* is the only goal; that is, the mystic experience, rather than adjunct to the primary mode of religiosity, is at the very center. Buddhism has to create theoretical reasons for its very own continuation. If the goal is the end of *samsāra*, then why would one who achieves release from it bother with teaching about it? If one realizes that not only is life an illusion but so is oneself and everyone else, then who is there to teach or to do the teaching? Would not religion then be a farce or a fraud?

The only answer is compassion. For while *samsāra* may be an illusion, for those stuck in it, suffering does take place. Illusory though it may be, it is still suffering. So Gautama Buddha taught what he had realized and what he understood as the most effective means to achieve enlightenment. And if one feels sorry for others who are suffering, one does all one can to end their suffering. Buddhism not only introduced monasticism to the world, it also introduced proselytizing. People had to be convinced that not only were they suffering, but there was a way out. In one of the early sutras, a parable of a burning house with children inside is presented. To convince them to leave, one tells them one has candy waiting for them outside, although one actually does not have any. The lie is but an expedient method to save them. Hence, as ordinary people need to worship, need objects of worship, need ritual, and so forth, so Buddhism was more than willing to fulfill these needs if it started people on the path to attaining *nirvāna*, a journey that may take many (illusory) lifetimes to complete. Buddhism is far from empty of paradox.

Compassion became so central to Buddhism that a major development, called Mahayana, created the notion of the Boddhisattva (Wisdom-being), one who could leave but remained in the world of illusion due to compassion for others. All Mahayana Buddhists take the Boddhisattva vow: that they will not allow themselves to enter *nirvāna* until all living entities have done so. From the theoretical perspective, this assumes that everyone eventually will have the experience, and it means that having the mystic experience commits one to help others to have the same experience. But, as with *darshan* in Hinduism, on the popular level, it was understood that such persons had spiritual merit that could be used for others. Boddhisattvas could be prayed to for succor; they became in effect quasi-deities.

Buddhist missionaries traveled throughout Asia, and Buddhism spread through Central, East, and Southeast Asia. Only the Mahayana forms of Buddhism, which were more open to modification and synthesis, survived in the more northern areas, becoming modified to both fit into a variety of cultural situations, as well as climatic and other differences from South Asia. Hence, in East Asia, Buddhism became amalgamated with familism, religion in which the central focus is the clan in and of itself, and in Central Asia, including Tibet and Mongolia, it became amalgamated with a shamanism that incorporates elements of mediumism.

Buddhism, due to its monastic underpinnings, became highly institutionalized. In China, as the monastaries became economic powerhouses, Buddhism competed with the state for power, and the state retaliated with major suppressions (not persecutions, as the concern was purely with institutional economic and political power, not with individual beliefs and practices, as is the case with the Falun Gong today). In Tibet, Buddhism became the state, with powerful, often competing, monasteries exercising feudal control over the areas surrounding them. For many monks, socioeconomic power became far more important than experiencing the bliss of nothingness.

Chinese religion, from at least the late Neolithic period over four thousand years ago, was centered on clan, that is, a family extended in both time and space. The primary ritual was the sacrificial offering of food to the important deceased members of the clan and the deceased of one's family. Parallel offering were made to cosmic and nature spirits, and much later in Chinese history, to anthropomorphic deities, who were understood as nonfamily dead humans with particular powers. Communication with the dead and deities was through various modes of divination and mediumistic spirit possession. This religious complex continues in the present; indeed, it defines Chinese culture. Other than functional mediumistic and shamanistic ecstasies, ecstatic experiences were not perceived to have a direct connection with normative religion as described.

Hence, those who had the mystic experience understood it to be a highly significant experience, one that gave one insight into reality as well as bliss, but an experience that was irrelevant to normative religiosity. Therefore, there was no tension between the mystic experience and religious practices, since they were understood as entirely separate activities and sets of understandings. And, accordingly, there was no systematization of the mystic experience. Aside from parts of three classic texts—the *Zhuangzi*, the *Daodejing*, and the *Liezi*—the experience was primarily dealt with in poetry, brushwork, and other modes of elite aesthetic expression.

Terminology that seems to have originally stemmed from the mystic experience was utilized in other endeavors, such as political philosophy, but with these developments, the terms lost their original relationship to the experience. So too terms stemming from the experience became used with regard to a secondary religious interest among the elite in China, the search for longevity. Opposite to the South Asian perspective on life, life in China was understood to be finite, and the longer it could be continued, so long as one lived a lifestyle worth continuing, the better. This was particularly important in a family-oriented society where only the eldest of the family, male and female, had a chance for independence. To be sure, there was an understanding that life continued after death, with one soul underground, the repository of the corpse, and one soul in the sky, where it merged with the other souls of the clan. But this continuation was not the same as life on earth and certainly not as desirable. Thus extending life was far more important to the elite than the occasional, hit-or-miss mystic experience. But to those who had the experience, to spend all one's energies on technology (alchemy, etc.) to extend life was meaningless, since only nothingness was real. Nonetheless, so long as we are alive, we might as well effortlessly enjoy it. Su Shi (194–96, see chapter 5) summed up this understanding in his "Red Cliff Prose-poem No. 1," dated to 1082:

> . . . My friend, do you understand the water and the moon? The first streams past yet is never gone; the second waxes and wanes eternally yet finally never increases nor diminishes. If you look from the standpoint of change, Sky and Earth do not last for even a blink of the eye, but if you look from the standpoint

of changelessness, that within and without ourselves are inexhaustible. So why should we envy anything?

Moreover, each thing between Sky and Earth has its owner; even a single hair which is not mine can never be a part of me. Only the cool breeze on the river and the full moon over the mountains caught by the ear becomes sound and encountered by the eye becomes color. No one can prevent us from having them, and there is no limit to our use of them. These are the limitless reserves of all that is created, and you and I can share in the joy of it.

Nevertheless, the search for longevity, along with cosmic renewal rituals, and rituals to assist the dead to enter a more desirable life after death, became amalgamated nearly two millennia ago in Daoism as an institutionalized religion. There are several lineages and styles of Daoism, but all exist in China not as separate religions but as adjunct to normative Chinese religion. In China, the only persons termed Daoists are hereditary, initiated priests or monks and nuns of the Quanzhen and other sects. While Daoism incorporates many of the terms in the previously mentioned Chinese texts that refer to the mystic experience, it is the terminology that is utilized, not the experience in and of itself. In China, the mystic experience remains essentially a nonreligious, from the institutional standpoint, experience, save for aspects of Chinese Buddhism.

So too Buddhism, which perhaps instigated the development of Daoism as a church, developed alongside Daoism in China. Those highly sinified forms that survived the various suppressions of an essentially foreign tradition had two foci, to be found in two sects. In Pure Land Buddhism, the focus was on achieving the placement of the sky soul of the deceased into the Western Paradise, a pleasant realm free of all of the entanglements of the living. Hence, this sect fit well into the Chinese familism, adding one more layer to the rituals for the family dead. Chan (Japanese: Zen) Buddhism initially focused on the mystic experience as did early Buddhism, which Chan understood to simply happen, and the less one strived to attain it, the better. Later, Chan too institutionalized practices to achieve realization of one's true nature of mind (which is no-mind), practices which in and of themselves may have been counter-productive for the mystic experience but facilitated the consciousness-only experience. Chan Buddhism remained another way in China to conceive and deal with the mystic experience, similar to the three classic Daoist texts that were familiar to all of the educated, especially as Chan did not posit the need to become a monk or nun, as other forms of Buddhism tended to do.

Differing from India, those who have the experience in China are much more likely to not speak of it, and they certainly will not become a charismatic focus for those seeking a vicarious enlightenment. The first line of the *Daodejing*—"The Dao that can be spoken of is not the eternal Dao"—as well as the lines, "The one who speaks does not know; the one who knows does not speak," tends to be taken seriously. Among those in China who have had the experience with whom I have spoken, whether Daoist monks, respected mediums, or literati artists, the experience was simply acknowledged, and then only in intimate conversations, for there was in actuality nothing about the experience that can be talked about.

For the development of mysticism in the West, Plotinus is instructive. Although he emphasizes union experiences with a null singularity, utilizing such terms as "the Supreme," "the One," and "God," he remains a Hellenistic polytheist. Thus, there is no discomfort nor the use of circuitous language to discuss unitive experiences with the One that is the sum and source of everything. In contrast, the Religions of the Book, particularly Christianity, has had to invent various circumlocutions, such as "the Godhead," to avoid contradicting their monotheistic theologies.

While the Religions of the Book are uncomfortable with a union experience because it denies a basic theological distinction between creator and created, they still must come to terms with an ecstatic union experience, for the experience cannot be denied by those who have it, and it simply will not go away within these religious traditions.

Although this is a controversial understanding of the past, I am under the impression that until the influence of modernity, the Kabbalah was commonly studied by Jews after the mastery of Talmud. That is, study of Kabbalah did not begin until around the age of forty after several decades of Talmud-Torah study, but it was commonly studied. Kabbalah study does not emphasize union experience, but it does concern itself with exoteric and esoteric spiritual practices. And among those involved in such practices, there will be those who have the mystic experience. Contrary to such scholars as Scholem, the Kabbalah and, in eastern Europe, the following Hasidic traditions, incorporated union experiences rather than deny them. Perhaps the differences among modern Jewish scholars as to their acceptance or denial of the experience in Judaism is based on their own spiritual experiences or lack thereof.

In Europe, after Napoleon, Jews were able to attain citizenship in some countries. Particularly in Germany, Jews entered the mainstream, and, in doing so, sought to harmonize their religion with the dominant Lutheran tradition of northern Germany. They dismissed the entire mystical stream of Judaism, which remained viable in the rural parts of eastern Europe via a generalized Hasidism until the Holocaust. Judaism in the United States and Canada was influenced by the developments in Germany until the shattered survivors of the Holocaust straggled in. Among the majority, throughout the different developing sects of Judaism, the tendency was to embrace form without content; ecstatic experience was a subject understood to be best ignored, if not denied. The study of the Kabbalah virtually disappeared, to resurface at the end of the twentieth century in a New Age guise.

Hasidic communities also became established in North America, but, in the main, it is a Hasidism at odds with the legendary spirituality of its foundational figure, the Baal-Shem (see Buber). Some Hasidic sects consider the garb of eighteenth-century Polish rent collectors of spiritual significance and rigidly adhere to it, even in the heat of Israel. And some give up individual spiritual development toward virtual worship of a zaddik, a leader with divine overtones. In other words, there is a tendency toward fundamentalism and loss of individuality, both of which are inimical to embracing the mystic experience. Similar to aspects of Hinduism, within Hasidism, there are those who seek a vicarious ecstasy through proximity with one understood as virtually divine, the zaddik.

Hence, save for new developments with small memberships, such as the Renewal movement, Jews seeking a spiritual life are caught in a dilemma between the horns of spiritual aridity and fundamentalism. It is hardly surprising that those of Jewish background seeking a spiritual life are among the forefront of those who have embraced Asian religions in North America or New Age movements.

Christianity too has a complex relationship with the mystic experience. Eastern Orthodoxy understands the experience to be the ultimate Christian one, while Roman Catholicism actively sought and continues to seek to suppress it among all but a few monks and nuns sequestered from contact with ordinary believers. Catholic students of mine who had the experience and sought advice from their priest invariably were counseled to put such experiences aside. Some were advised to pray to be free from such experiences, while it was suggested to others they seek psychiatric treatment. Contemporary priests who have refused to remain silent about the experience and what one learns from it have been defrocked. These anecdotal situations are corroborated by the findings of the National Opinion Research

Center survey discussed in chapter 4. The number of Catholics who reported religious experiences was significantly less, from the statistical standpoint, than for any other designated religious group, including those who labeled themselves as having no religious affiliation. This does not mean that Catholics are not having the experiences as frequently as others but that they are not considering the experiences religious due to their enculturation in this regard. Unfortunately, there was no category for Eastern Orthodoxy to ascertain if indeed there was a higher incidence of reports as the Church's orientation would lead us to expect.

American Protestantism had surges of fervid spirituality in the mid-nineteenth century, but most of the larger denominations moved away from spiritual experiences to sedate, short Sunday morning gatherings, where dignified behavior was valued over ecstasy. Instead, "secular" spiritual practices, such as Spiritualism, developed in the late nineteenth century to fill the void. Bucke is a prime example of the secularization of the mystic experience in the Western world. Trained in the science of medicine, rather than associate his experience with one of the Religions of the Book, he understood his union to have been with a vague cosmic entity not called "God."

In Islam, an early development was the Sufi tradition, which centers on personal religious experiences, often ecstatic. In Turkey, which became the homeland of several Sufi traditions, this aspect of Islam was declared illegal in the early part of the twentieth century, but it still flourishes even there. The Ismaili tradition also emphasizes personal religious experiences and is considerably more inclusive of females than Islam in general.

The effects of the Enlightenment were to turn people away from enlightenment. Science was understood to be opposite to religion, and only conscious reasoning was given any credence. Ecstatic experiences, hence, were anathema, and having them was a sign of mental dysfunction. The proper place for mystics were insane asylums; although now, pharmaceutical drugs are the favored means of curing persons from having ecstasies. The mainstream churches moved away from any practices that would encourage spiritual fervor. Christian and Jewish scholars began to focus on literary studies of the Bible and archaeology to understand their religions instead of the traditional spirituality. What was ignored was that many leading scientists, such as Einstein, saw no disparity between spirituality and science, and that all scientific breakthroughs require nonconscious mental activity, often ecstatic. The unconscious undoubtedly has been used to solve problems since the first humans.

During the latter part of the twentieth-century, charismatic movements began in particular Protestant sects and in Roman Catholicism, but these movements had little influence among the mainstream churches. Instead, the only Christian denomination demonstrating growth, and a rapid growth at that, has been Pentecostalism, which expects its adherents to have ecstatic experiences. Pentecostal churches generally require one to be baptized by the Holy Spirit, that is, to have an intense ecstatic experience, some being the mystic experience, to be a full member of the Church. Yet, Pentecostalism is intimately wedded to Christian Fundamentalism, requiring a literal interpretation of the Bible and the spurning of the religious significance of myth, thus stilling the intellect and the imagination. This, in turn, turns away those who are broadly educated and oriented toward intellectual pursuits. Hence, the New Age movements.

Psychologists and psychiatrists who did understand ecstatic behavior from a positive perspective, particularly those that utilized psychoactive substances in the mid-twentieth century in their work (such as Grof); anthropologists familiar with non-Western shamanistic practices (such as Harner); persons who modernized the Theosophic bent to receive teachings in trance, now not from millennium-old seers in the Himalayas, but from outer space or sunken continents; ersatz shamans who falsely claimed training by Native American or Siberian healers; hawkers of crystals and esoteric oils, in combination with modern consumerism, generated the New Age. Now seekers of spiritual experience have a panoply of evening and weekend workshops from which to choose. In a single weekend, often for a substantial fee, they can become a shaman, engage in supposed Native American rituals and gain a Native name, learn to heal with crystals, restore their true feminine nature, or any number of other overtly worthwhile spiritual growth opportunities.

One can be taught to have a shamanistic-type experience in a short period of time, since virtually all humans can, for example, travel while in trance, if they but allow themselves to. But, experiencing the void is something else. No religious tradition has been successful in doing this, even after twenty or more years of training. One can be assisted in having visions, in gaining an experience of total well-being, in helping others in various ways, and so on, although not necessarily in a weekend. But the mystic experience cannot be bought, cannot be taught, cannot even be sought. It happens.

SUMMARY

Thus, there is an experience, an ecstatic experience of nothingness or complete unity, in which the self disappears in bliss, often deemed mysterious and exceedingly rare, that actually many people have had. Cultures can integrate the mystic experience in a variety of ways. For shamanistic and mediumistic traditions, the mystic experience is understood as a highly personal experience that, at most, is but tangentially related to functional ecstatic experiences; they are not important to the culture per se.

In Hinduism, the mystic experience has been integrated into religion as one of four ends to living a full life, although for most, the experience is assumed to be gained vicariously through being in the presence of one who is understood to have had such an experience. Buddhism was formed with the mystic experience at its core, but increasing institutionalization theoretically puts the experience further and further out of the reach of adherents. I have encountered Buddhists who imparted their ecstatic experience to Buddhist masters who informed them that their experience could not be valid because they were not high enough up in the hierarchy to have had it. In China, the experience is not correlated with normative religious behavior, but traditionally, among the elite, it was a highly valued, although little discussed, experience.

The Religions of the Book have far from a consistent reaction to the experience. The modernization of Judaism in the main could be interpreted as virtually denying the experience, although Jews of varying degrees of relationship to the tradition, of course, have the experience in any case. Christianity ranges from mainstream Protestantism, which often considers those who have the experience to be mentally ill unfortunates, to Catholicism, which accepts the experience, but only for a few who are sequestered from the laity, to Orthodoxy, which considers the experience to be the quintessence of the Christian life, to Pentecostalism, which welcomes, even expects, the mystic or other ecstatic experience for full membership. Then there are contemporary developments that fall within the rubric of "New Age," some of which seek to commercialize the experience, capitalizing on those with a lifestyle in which individuals with disposable income but limited time hope to find the ultimate in a weekend—another modern concept. The Sufi tradition within Islam fully accepts the mystic experience and fosters practices that are thought to facilitate it, but it is understood that it is best not to speak about intensely personal religious experiences.

But all of the above examples of the mystic experience when institutionalized often tend to be perceived as limited to adherents of one's particular institution. Thus the experiences that others have may be understood as false, or, if understood as related, to be somehow lesser than the experiences available within the institution. Nonetheless, given the huge human population, even if far less than 10 percent of the population has had the experience, that is still an enormous number, many millions of people. Some of you reading this book will have had it. I trust you now understand that you are not crazy but blessed. For those of you who have not had the mystic experience but wish to have it, do not be frustrated. There is little you can do to attain it, but the more relaxed you are about it and the less you want it, the more likely you are to experience it. And now, if you do, I trust it will no longer be a mystery, that you will realize what is happening and simply let go and allow yourself to disappear in bliss.

Works Consulted

Alston, William P. "Ineffability." *The Philosophical Review* 65 (1956): 506–22.

Anand, B. K., G. S. Chhina, and Baldev Singh. "Some Aspects of Electroencephalographic Studies in Yogis." *Electroencephalographic Clinical Neurophysiology* 13 (1961): 452–56.

Arbman, Ernst. *Ecstasy or Religious Trance: In the Experience of the Ecstatics and from the Psychological Point of View.* 3 vol. Ed. Åke Hultkrantz. Upsalla: Scandinavian University Books, 1963, 1968, 1970.

Austin, James H. *Zen and the Brain: Toward an Understanding of Meditation and Consciousness.* Cambridge: Massachusetts Institute of Technology Press, 1998.

Bäckman, Louise and Åke Hultkrantz. *Studies in Lapp Shamanism.* Stockholm Series in Comparative Religion 16 (1978).

Barnard, G. William. *Exploring Unseen Worlds: William James and the Philosophy of Mysticism.* Albany: State University of New York Press, 1997.

Bharati, Agehananda. *The Ochre Robe: An Autobiography.* London: George Allen & Unwin, 1961.

———. *The Light at the Center: Context and Pretext of Modern Mysticism.* Santa Barbara: Ross Erickson, 1976.

Bhattacharya, Sutapas. *The Oneness/Otherness Mystery: The Synthesis of Science and Mysticism.* Delhi: Motilal Banarsidass, 1999.

Blakney, Raymond Bernard. Translator. *Meister Eckhart: A Modern Translation.* New York: Harper Torchbooks, 1957.

Boehme, Jacob. *Six Theosophic Points and Other Writings.* Trans. John R. Earle. Ann Arbor: University of Michigan Press, 1958.

Buber, Martin. *The Legend of the Baal-Shem*. Princeton: Princeton University Press, 1955.

Bucke, Richard Maurice. *Cosmic Consciousness: A Study in the Evolution of the Human Mind*. Secaucus, N.J.: Citadel Press, 1961 (1900).

Bush, Susan. *The Chinese Literati on Painting*. Cambridge: Harvard University Press, 1971.

Chang Chung-yüan. *Creativity and Taoism*. New York: The Julian Press, 1963.

Chaves, Jonathan. "The Legacy of Ts'ang Chieh: The Written Word as Magic." *Oriental Art* 23 (1977): 200–15.

Chen Meng-jia. "Shangdai de shenhau yu wushu," *Yenjing xuebao* 20 (1936): 555–59.

Chittick, William C. *The Sufi Path of Love: The Spiritual Teachings of Rumi*. Albany: State University of New York Press, 1983.

Clarke, Arthur C. *Childhood's End*. New York: Ballantine Books, 1953.

Colledge, Edmund and Bernard McGinn. Translators. *Meister Eckhart: The Essential Commentaries, Treatises and Defense*. New York: Paulist Press, 1981.

Concordance to Chuang Tzu, A. Harvard-Yenching Institute Sinological Index Series, Supplement No. 20. Cambridge: Harvard University Press, 1947.

Conze, Edward. Editor. *Buddhist Texts Through the Ages*. Oxford: Bruno Cassirer, 1954.

———. *Selected Sayings from the Perfection of Wisdom*. London: The Buddhist Society, 1955.

———. *Buddhist Meditation*. London: George Allen & Unwin, 1956.

———. Unpublished "Lists of Buddhist Terms," 1963.

d'Aquili, Eugene G. and Charles D. Laughlin. "The Neurobiology of Myth and Ritual." *The Spectrum of Ritual, A Biogenic Structural Analysis*. Ed. G. d'Aquili, Charles D. Laughlin Jr., and John McManus. New York: Columbia University Press, 1979.

d'Aquili, Eugene G. and Andrew B. Newberg. *The Mystical Mind: Probing the Biology of Religious Experience*. Minneapolis: Fortress Press, 1999.

de Bary, Theodore Wm. General Editor. *Sources of Indian Tradition*. vol. 1. New York: Columbia University Press, 1958.

de Mille, Richard. *Castaneda's Journey: The Power and the Allegory*. Santa Barbara: Capra Press, 1976.

Deikman, Arthur J. "Implications of Experimentally Induced Contemplative Meditation." *The Journal of Nervous and Mental Disease* 142 (1966): 101–16.

———. "Deautomatization and the Mystic Experience." *Psychiatry* 29 (1966): 324–38.

Desani, G. V. *All About H. Hatter.* New York: Lancer Books, 1972.

DeWoskin, Kenneth J. *Doctors, Diviners, and Magicians: Biographies of "Fang-shih."* New York: Columbia University Press, 1983.

Dupré, Louis and James A. Wiseman. *Light from Light: An Anthology of Christian Mysticism.* New York: Paulist Press, 1988.

Edsman, Carl-Martin. Editor. *Studies in Shamanism.* Stockholm: Scripta Instituti Donnerieani Abensis 1, 1962.

Ehrenreich, Barbara. "Hey—You With the Cheese on Your Head: Are We Searching for Ecstasy in All the Wrong Places?" *Time*, January 26, 1998: 60.

Eliade, Mircea. *Shamanism: Archaic Techniques of Ecstasy.* Trans. Willard R. Trask. Princeton: Princeton University Press (Bollingen Series 76), 1964.

Elior, Rachel. *The Paradoxical Ascent to God: The Kabbalistic Theosophy of Habad Hasidism.* Albany: State University of New York Press, 1993.

Eskildsen, Stephen. "Seeking Signs of Proof: Visions and Other Trance Phenomena in Early Quanzhen Taoism," *Journal of Chinese Religions* 29 (2001): 139–60.

Forman, Robert K. C. *Mysticism, Mind, Consciousness.* Albany: State University of New York Press, 1999.

Freud, Sigmund. *Civilization and Its Discontents.* Trans. Joan Rivere. London: Hogarth Press, 1930.

Furst, Peter T. Editor. *Flesh of the Gods: The Ritual Use of Hallucinogens.* New York: Praeger, 1972.

Gale, Richard M. "Mysticism and Philosophy." *The Journal of Philosophy* 57 (1960): 471–81.

Gallup, George Jr. *Adventures in Immortality.* New York: McGraw-Hill, 1977.

Gillet, Archminadrite Lev. *The Jesus Prayer.* Crestwood, N.Y.: St. Vladimir's Press, 1987.

Gilson, Étienne. *The Mystical Theology of Saint Bernard.* Trans. A. H. C. Downes, 1940. London: Sheed and Ward.

Ginsburg, Elliot K. *The Sabbath in the Classical Kabbalah.* Albany: State University of New York Press, 1989.

Graham, A. C. "Chuang-Tzu and the Rambling Mode." *The Art and Profession of Translation.* Ed. T. C. Lai. Hong Kong: The Hong Kong Translation Society, n.d.

———. "The Date and Composition of Liehtzyy." *Asia Major* N.S. 8 (1961): 139–98.

———. "Chuang-tzu's Essay on Seeing Things as Equal." *History of Religions* 9 (1967): 137–59.

———. "How Much of *Chuang Tzu* did Chuang Tzu Write?" *Studies in Chinese Classical Thought.* Ed. Henry Rosemont Jr. and Benjamin I. Schwartz. *Journal of the American Academy of Religion, Thematic Issue* 47/3S (1979): 459–502.

Greeley, Andrew M. *The Sociology of the Paranormal: A Reconnaissance.* Beverly Hills, Calif.: Sage Publications, 1975.

Grof, Stanislav. *The Cosmic Game: Explorations of the Frontiers of Human Consciousness.* Albany: State University of New York Press, 1998.

———. *Psychology of the Future: Lessons from Modern Consciousness Research.* Albany: State University of New York Press, 2000.

Hallowell, A. Irving. "Ojibwa Ontology, Behavior, and World View." *Culture in History: Essays in Honor of Paul Radin.* Ed. Stanley Diamond. New York: Columbia University Press, 1960: 19–52.

Hanegraaff, Wouter J. *New Age Religion and Western Culture: Esotericism in the Mirror of Secular Thought.* Albany: State University of New York Press, 1998.

Happold, F. C. *Mysticism: A Study and an Anthology.* New York: Penguin, 1963.

Hardy, Alister. *The Spiritual Nature of Man.* London: Oxford University Press, 1979.

Harner, Michael J. *The Jivaro: People of the Sacred Waterfall.* New York: Natural History Press, 1972.

———. Editor. *Hallucinogens and Shamanism.* London: Oxford University Press, 1973.

———. *The Way of the Shaman: A Guide to Power and Healing.* San Francisco: Harper & Row, 1980.

Hawkes, David. *Ch'u Tz'u: The Songs of the South.* London: Oxford University Press, 1959.

Hesse, Hermann. *Magister Ludi (The Bead Game).* Trans. Mervyn Savill. New York: Frederick Unger, 1949.

Hightower, James R. "Ch'u Yüan Studies." *Silver Jubilee Volume of the Zinbun-Kagaku-Kenkyusyo.* Kyoto: Kyoto University, 1954.

————. *The Poetry of T'ao Ch'ien*. Oxford: Oxford University Press, 1970.

Ho P'ing-ti. *The Cradle of the East*. Chicago: University of Chicago Press, 1975.

Hoffman, Helmut. *Symbolik der Tibetischen Religionen und des Shamanismus*. Stuttgart: Anton Hiersmann, 1967.

Hsü Cho-yun. *Ancient China in Transition, An Analysis of Social Mobility, 722–222 B.C.* Stanford: Stanford University Press, 1965.

Hultkrantz, Åke. "A Definition of Shamanism." *Temenos* 9 (1973): 25–37.

Hume, Robert Ernest. *The Thirteen Principal Upanishads*. second ed. London: Oxford University Press, 1931 (1877).

Huxley, Aldous. *The Perennial Philosophy*. London: Chatto & Windus, 1946.

Idel, Moshe. *Kabbalah: New Perspectives*. New Haven: Yale University Press, 1988.

————. *The Mystical Experience in Abraham Abulafia*. Albany: State University of New York Press, 1988.

————. "Universalization and Integration: Two Conceptions of Mystical Union in Jewish Mysticism." *Mystical Union and Monotheistic Faith: An Ecumenical Dialogue*. Ed. Moshe Idel and Bernard McGinn. New York: MacMillan, 1989.

————. *Hasidism: Between Ecstasy and Magic*. Albany: State University of New York Press, 1995.

James, William. *The Varieties of Religious Experience*. New York: New American Library, 1958 (1902).

Jenness, Diamond. *The Ojibwa Indians of Parry Island: Their Social and Religious Life*. Ottawa: National Museum of Canada, 1936.

Jilek, Wolfgang G. *Salish Indian Mental Health and Culture Change: Psychohygienic and Therapeutic Aspects of the Guardian Spirit Ceremonial*. Toronto: Holt, Rinehart and Winston, 1974.

John of the Cross, St. *Dark Night of the Soul*. Trans. A. Allison Peers. New York: Image Books, 1959.

Johnson, Marilyn E. "Shamanic 'Flight' Analysis and Comparison to the *Ch'u Tz'u*." Unpublished paper. Toronto: York University, 1978. (Reproduced with permission of the author with minor editing by J. Paper.)

Jones, Richard H. *Mysticism Examined: Philosophical Inquiries into Mysticism*. Albany: State University of New York Press, 1993.

Kasamatsu, Ikira and Tomio Hirai. "An Electroencephalographic Study on the Zen Meditation (Zazen)." *Folio Psychiatrica et Neurologica Japonica* 20 (1966): 315–36.

Katz, Steven T. "Language, Epistomology, and Mysticism." *Mysticism and Philo-sophical Analysis*. Ed. Steven T. Katz. London: Sheldon Press, 1978.

Kendall, Laurel. *Shamans, Housewives, and Other Restless Spirits: Women in Korean Religious Life*. Honolulu: University of Hawaii Press, 1985.

Kohn, Livia. "Guarding the One: Concentrative Meditation in Taoism." *Taoist Meditation and Longevity Techniques*. Ed. Livia Kohn. Ann Arbor: Center for Chinese Studies, The University of Michigan, 1989.

Kripal, Jeffery J. *Roads of Excess, Palaces of Wisdom: Eroticism and Reflexivity in the Study of Mysticism*. Chicago: University of Chicago Press, 2001.

Krivocheine, Archbishop Basil. *In the Light of Christ: Saint Symeon the New Theolo-gian (949–1022)*. Trans. Anthony P. Gythiel. Crestwood, N.Y.: St. Vladimir's Seminary Press, 1986.

Laing, R. D. *The Politics of Experience*. New York: Pantheon Books, 1967.

Landes, Ruth. *Ojibwa Religion and the Midewiwin*. Madison: University of Wisconsin Press, 1968.

———. *The Prairie Potawatomi: Tradition and Ritual in the Twentieth Century*. Madison: University of Wisconsin Press, 1970.

Laughlin, Charles D. Jr., John McManus, and Eugene G. d'Aquili. *Brain, Symbol and Experience: Towards of Neurophenomenology of Human Consciousness*. Boston: Shambhala, 1990.

Lefcoe, Yaacov. *Sharing* teshuva *Wisdom: Judaically-informed Psychotherapeutic Coun-selling of* 'baal teshuva' *Returnees to Judaism*. Toronto: York University, unpub-lished master's thesis, Graduate Program in Psychology, Clinical Area, 1998.

Lewis, I. M. *Ecstatic Religion: An Anthropological Study of Spirit Possession and Shaman-ism*. Baltimore: Penguin, 1971.

Lewis, James R. and Gordon J. Melton. Editors. *Perspectives on the New Age*. Albany: State University of New York Press, 1992.

Lin Yutang. *The Gay Genius*. New York: John Day, 1947.

Lommel, Andreas. *Shamanism: The Beginnings of Art*. Trans. by Michael Bullock. New York: McGraw-Hill, 1967.

Lossky, Vladimir. *The Mystical Theology of the Eastern Church*. Trans. unspecified. Crestwood, N.Y.: St. Vladimir's Seminary Press, 1976 (1944).

Lowie, Robert H. *An Introduction to Anthropology*. New York. Rinehart, 1940.

Ludwig, Arnold M. "Altered States of Consciousness." *Archives of General Psychiatry* 15 (1966): 225–34.

Lundhal, Craig R. and Harold A. Widdison. *The Eternal Journey: How Near-Death Experiences Illuminate Our Earthly Lives*. New York: Warner Books, 1997.

Mandell, Arnold J. "Toward a Psychobiology of Transcendence: God in the Brain." *The Psychobiology of Consciousness*. Ed. Julian M. Davidson and Richard J. Davidson. New York: Plenum, 1980.

Maslow, Abraham H. *Religions, Values, and Peak-Experiences*. Middlesex, England: Penguin Press, 1964.

Mather, Richard B. "The Controversy over Conformity and Naturalness During the Six Dynasties," *History of Religions* 9 (1969): 159–80.

Merkur, Daniel. *Becoming Half Hidden: Shamanism and Initiation Among the Inuit*. Stockholm Studies in Comparative Religion 24, 1985.

———. *The Ecstatic Imagination: Psychedelic Experience and the Psychoanalysis of Self-Actualization*. Albany: State University of New York Press, 1998.

———. *Mystical Moments and Unitive Thinking*. Albany: State University of New York Press, 1999.

———. *The Mystery of Manna: The Psychodelic Sacrament of the Bible*. Rochester, Vermont: Park Street Press, 2000.

Moody, Raymond Jr. *Life after Life*. New York: Bantam Books, 1975.

Otto, Rudolph. *Mysticism East and West: A Comparative Analysis of the Nature of Mysticism*. Trans. Bertha L. Bracey and Richenda C. Payne. New York: MacMillan, 1932.

Owens, J., E. Cook, and I. Stevenson. "Features of Near-Death Experience in Relation to Whether or Not Patients Were Near Death." *Lancet* 336 (1990): 1175–77.

Paper, Jordan. "The Early Development of Chinese Cosmology," *Chinese Culture* 15/2 (1974): 15–25.

———. *The Fu-tzu: A Post-Han Confucian Text*. Leiden: E. J. Brill, Monographies du T'oung Pao, vol. 13, 1987.

———. "'Sweat Lodge': A Northern Native American Ritual for Communal Shamanic Trance." *Temenos* 26 (1990): 85–94.

———. *The Spirits Are Drunk: Comparative Approaches to Chinese Religion*. Albany: State University of New York Press, 1995.

———. "Mediums and Modernity: The Institutionalization of Ecstatic Religious Functionaries in Taiwan." *Journal of Chinese Religions* 24 (1996): 105–30.

———. *Through the Earth Darkly: Female Spirituality in Comparative Perspective*. New York: Continuum, 1997.

Patai, Raphael. *The Jewish Alchemists: A History and Sourcebook*. Princeton: Princeton University Press, 1994.

Pelletier, Wilfrid and Ted Poole. *No Foreign Land: The Biography of a North American Indian*. Toronto: McClelland and Stewart, 1973.

Plotinus. *The Enneads*. Trans. Stephen MacKenna. Third ed. rev. by B. S. Page. London: Faber and Faber, 1956.

Proudfoot, Wayne. *Religious Experience*. Berkeley: University of California Press, 1985.

Radin, Paul. "An Introductive Enquiry in the Study of Ojibwa Religion." *Papers and Records of the Ontario Historical Society*. vol. 12, 1914.

———. "Ojibwa and Ottawa Puberty Dreams." *Essays in Anthropology Presented to A. L. Kroeber*. Ed. R. H. Lowie. Berkeley: University of California Press, 1936.

Rasmussen, Knut. *Thulefahrt*. Frankfurt-am-Main: 1925.

Roberts, G., and J. Owen. "The Near-Death Experience." *British Journal of Psychiatry* 153 (1988): 607–17.

Rogers, Edward S. *The Round Lake Ojibwa*. Toronto: Royal Ontario Museum, 1962.

———. "Natural Environment-Social Organization-Witchcraft: Cree Versus Ojibwa—A Test Case." *Contributions to Anthropology: Ecological Essays*. Ed. David Damas. Ottawa: National Museums of Canada, 1969.

Rouget, Gilbert. *Music and Trance: A Theory of the Relations between Music and Possession*. Trans. Brunhilde Biebuyck. Chicago: University of Chicago Press, 1985.

Schafer, Edward H. *The Divine Woman, Dragon Ladies and Rain Maidens in T'ang Literature*. Berkeley: University of California Press, 1973.

Scholem, Gershom G. *Major Trends in Jewish Mysticism*. New York: Schocken Books, 1941.

———. *Origins of the Kaballah*. Ed. R. J. Werblowsky. Trans. Allan Arkush. New York: Jewish Publication Society, 1987 (1962).

Seidel, Anna K. *La divinisation de Lau Tseu dans le Taoisme des Han*. Paris: Ecole Française d'Extreme-Orient, 1969.

Sells, Michael A. "Bewildered Tongue: The Semantics of Mystical Union in Islam." *Mystical Union and Monotheistic Faith: An Ecumenical Dialogue.* Ed. Moshe Idel and Bernard McGinn. New York: MacMillan, 1989.

———. *Mystical Languages of Unsaying.* Chicago: University of Chicago Press, 1994.

———. *Early Islamic Mysticism: Sufi, Qur'an, Mi'raj, Poetic and Theological Writings.* New York: Paulist Press, 1996.

Shankara. *Crest-Jewel of Discrimination (Viveka Chudamani).* Trans. Swami Prabhavananda and Christopher Isherwood. Los Angeles: Vedanta Society, 1947.

Sjørup, Lene. "Mysticism and Gender." *Journal of Feminist Studies in Religion* 13 (1997): 45–68.

Smart, Ninian. "Interpretation and Mystical Experience." *Religious Studies* 1 (1965): 75–87.

Staal, Fritz. *Exploring Mysticism.* Baltimore: Penguin, 1975.

Stace, W. T. *Mysticism and Philosophy.* Philadelphia: J. B. Lippincott, 1960.

Stanley-Baker, Joan. "The Development of Brush-Modes in Sung and Yüan." *Artibus Asiae* 39 (1977): 13–59.

Starbuck, E. D. *The Psychology of Religion.* New York: Scribner, 1899.

Stuckey, Johanna H. "Great Goddesses of the Ancient Levant." Bulletin *of the Canadian Society for Mesopotamian Studies* 37 (2002): 27–48.

Su Shi. "Red Cliff Fu 1." Trans. Jordan Paper. *The Chinese Way in Religion.* Second ed. Ed. Jordan Paper and Lawrence G. Thompson. Belmont, Calif.: Wadsworth, 1998.

Tart, Charles T. *Altered States of Consciousness: A Book of Readings.* New York: John Wiley & Sons, 1969.

———. *States of Consciousness.* New York: E. P. Dutton, 1974.

Thiel, P. Jos. "Schamanismus im Alten China." *Sinologica* 10 (1968): 149–204.

Travis, Frederick and Craig Pearson. "Pure Consciousness: Distinct Phenomenological and Psychological Correlates of 'Consciousness Itself.'" *International Journal of Neuroscience* 100 (2000): 77–89.

Underhill, Evelyn. *Mysticism: A Study in the Nature of Man's Spiritual Consciousness.* New York: Dutton, 1910.

van Gulik, Robert Hans. *The Lore of the Chinese Lute, An Essay in Ch'in Ideology.* Tokyo: Sophia University, 1940.

Ward, J. A. "The Wikwemikong Suicide Epidemic, A Psychiatric Analysis." Presented to the Coroner's Jury, December 11–12, 1975.

Ward, J. A. and Joseph Fox. "A Suicide Epidemic on an Indian Reserve." *Canadian Psychiatric Association Journal* 22/8 (1977): 423–26.

Warren, Henry Clarke. *Buddhism in Translations*. Cambridge: Harvard University Press, 1896.

Wasson, R. Gordon, Carl A. Ruck, and Albert Hofmann. *The Road to Eleusis: Unveiling the Secret of the Mysteries*. New York: Harcourt Brace Jovanovich, 1978.

Watts, Fraser. "Cognitive Neuroscience and Religious Consciousness." *Neuroscience and the Person: Scientific Perspectives on Divine Action*. Ed. John Robert Russell et al. Vatican City State: Vatican Observatory Publications, 1999: 326–46.

Weil, Andrew. *The Natural Mind: A New Way of Looking at Drugs and Higher Consciousness*. Boston: Houghton Mifflin, 1972.

White, Charles S. J. "Mother Guru: Jnanananda of Madras, India." *Unspoken Worlds: Women's Religious Lives*. Ed. Nancy Auer Falk and Rita M. Gross. Belmont, Calif.: Wadsworth Press, 1989: 15–24.

Wilber, Ken. *Eye to Eye: The Quest for the New Paradigm*. New York: Doubleday, 1983.

Wildman, Wesley J. and Leslie A. Brothers. "A Neuropsychological-Semiotic Model of Religious Experiences." *Neuroscience and the Person: Scientific Perspectives on Divine Action*. Ed. John Robert Russell et al. Vatican City State: Vatican Observatory Publications, 1999: 347–416.

Winkelman, Michael. "Trance States: A Theoretical Model and Cross-Cultural Analysis." *Ethos* 14 (1986): 174–203.

Winson, Jonathan. "The Meaning of Dreams." *Mysteries of the Mind. Scientific American* Special Issue 7 (1997): 58–67.

Wolfson, Elliot R. *Through a Speculum That Shines: Vision and Imagination in Medieval Jewish Mysticism*. Princeton: Princeton University Press, 1994.

Woods, Richard. Editor. *Understanding Mysticism*. Garden City, N.J.: Image Books, 1980.

Zaehner, R. C. *Mysticism: Sacred and Profane*. New York: Oxford University Press, 1957.

Zaleski, Carol. *Otherworld Journeys: Accounts of Near-Death Experience in Medieval and Modern Times*. New York: Oxford University Press, 1987.

Zinberg, N. "The Study of Consciousness States, Problems and Progress." *Alternate States of Consciousness*. Ed. N. Zinberg. New York: Free Press, 1977: 158–219.

Index

Printed in Great Britain
by Amazon

23328040R00106